Keep this book. You will need it and use it throughout your career.

About the American Hotel & Lodging Association (AH&LA)

Founded in 1910, AH&LA is the trade association representing the lodging industry in the United States. AH&LA is a federation of state lodging associations throughout the United States with 11,000 lodging properties worldwide as members. The association offers its members assistance with governmental affairs representation, communications, marketing, hospitality operations, training and education, technology issues, and more. For information, call 202-289-3100.

LODGING, the management magazine of AH&LA, is a "living textbook" for hospitality students that provides timely features, industry news, and vital lodging information.

About the American Hotel & Lodging Educational Institute (EI)

An affiliate of AH&LA, the Educational Institute is the world's largest source of quality training and educational materials for the lodging industry. EI develops textbooks and courses that are used in more than 1,200 colleges and universities worldwide, and also offers courses to individuals through its Distance Learning program. Hotels worldwide rely on EI for training resources that focus on every aspect of lodging operations. Industry-tested videos, CD-ROMs, seminars, and skills guides prepare employees at every skill level. EI also offers professional certification for the industry's top performers. For information about EI's products and services, call 800-349-0299 or 407-999-8100.

About the American Hotel & Lodging Educational Foundation (AH&LEF)

An affiliate of AH&LA, the American Hotel & Lodging Educational Foundation provides financial support that enhances the stability, prosperity, and growth of the lodging industry through educational and research programs. AH&LEF has awarded millions of dollars in scholarship funds for students pursuing higher education in hospitality management. AH&LEF has also funded research projects on topics important to the industry, including occupational safety and health, turnover and diversity, and best practices in the U.S. lodging industry. For more information, go to www.ahlef.org.

00374TXT01ENGE
PP-3545

REVENUE MANAGEMENT

Maximizing Revenue in Hospitality Operations

Revenue management
→ A.K.A. Yield management } one in the same.

is an operational approach that integrates:
financial
operations
marketing
with pricing.

Accepting the right business at the right time

Educational Institute Books

UNIFORM SYSTEM OF ACCOUNTS FOR THE LODGING INDUSTRY
Tenth Revised Edition

WORLD OF RESORTS: FROM DEVELOPMENT TO MANAGEMENT
Third Edition
Chuck Yim Gee

PLANNING AND CONTROL FOR FOOD AND BEVERAGE OPERATIONS
Seventh Edition
Jack D. Ninemeier

UNDERSTANDING HOSPITALITY LAW
Fifth Edition
Jack P. Jefferies/Banks Brown

SUPERVISION IN THE HOSPITALITY INDUSTRY
Fourth Edition
Raphael R. Kavanaugh/Jack D. Ninemeier

MANAGEMENT OF FOOD AND BEVERAGE OPERATIONS
Fifth Edition
Jack D. Ninemeier

MANAGING FRONT OFFICE OPERATIONS
Eighth Edition
Michael L. Kasavana/Richard M. Brooks

MANAGING SERVICE IN FOOD AND BEVERAGE OPERATIONS
Third Edition
Ronald F. Cichy/Philip J. Hickey, Jr.

THE LODGING AND FOOD SERVICE INDUSTRY
Seventh Edition
Gerald W. Lattin

SECURITY AND LOSS PREVENTION MANAGEMENT
Second Edition
Raymond C. Ellis, Jr./David M. Stipanuk

HOSPITALITY INDUSTRY MANAGERIAL ACCOUNTING
Sixth Edition
Raymond S. Schmidgall

PURCHASING FOR FOOD SERVICE OPERATIONS
Ronald F. Cichy/Jeffery D Elsworth

MANAGING TECHNOLOGY IN THE HOSPITALITY INDUSTRY
Fifth Edition
Michael L. Kasavana/John J. Cahill

BASIC HOTEL AND RESTAURANT ACCOUNTING
Sixth Edition
Raymond Cote

ACCOUNTING FOR HOSPITALITY MANAGERS
Fifth Edition
Raymond Cote

CONVENTION MANAGEMENT AND SERVICE
Eighth Edition
Milton T. Astroff/James R. Abbey

HOSPITALITY SALES AND MARKETING
Fifth Edition
James R. Abbey

MANAGING HOUSEKEEPING OPERATIONS
Revised Third Edition
Aleta A. Nitschke/William D. Frye

DIMENSIONS OF TOURISM
Joseph D. Fridgen

HOSPITALITY TODAY: AN INTRODUCTION
Seventh Edition
Rocco M. Angelo/Andrew N. Vladimir

HOSPITALITY FACILITIES MANAGEMENT AND DESIGN
Third Edition
David M. Stipanuk

07/10

MANAGING HOSPITALITY HUMAN RESOURCES
Fourth Edition
Robert H. Woods

RETAIL MANAGEMENT FOR SPAS

HOSPITALITY INDUSTRY FINANCIAL ACCOUNTING
Third Edition
Raymond S. Schmidgall/James W. Damitio

INTERNATIONAL HOTELS: DEVELOPMENT & MANAGEMENT
Second Edition
Chuck Yim Gee

QUALITY SANITATION MANAGEMENT
Ronald F. Cichy

HOTEL INVESTMENTS: ISSUES & PERSPECTIVES
Fourth Edition
Edited by Lori E. Raleigh and Rachel J. Roginsky

LEADERSHIP AND MANAGEMENT IN THE HOSPITALITY INDUSTRY
Third Edition
Robert H. Woods/Judy Z. King

MARKETING IN THE HOSPITALITY INDUSTRY
Fifth Edition
Ronald A. Nykiel

CONTEMPORARY HOSPITALITY MARKETING
William Lazer/Roger Layton

UNIFORM SYSTEM OF ACCOUNTS FOR THE HEALTH, RACQUET AND SPORTSCLUB INDUSTRY

CONTEMPORARY CLUB MANAGEMENT
Second Edition
Edited by Joe Perdue for the Club Managers Association of America

RESORT CONDOMINIUM AND VACATION OWNERSHIP MANAGEMENT: A HOSPITALITY PERSPECTIVE
Robert A. Gentry/Pedro Mandoki/Jack Rush

ACCOUNTING FOR CLUB OPERATIONS
Raymond S. Schmidgall/James W. Damitio

TRAINING AND DEVELOPMENT FOR THE HOSPITALITY INDUSTRY
Debra F. Cannon/Catherine M. Gustafson

UNIFORM SYSTEM OF FINANCIAL REPORTING FOR CLUBS
Sixth Revised Edition

HOTEL ASSET MANAGEMENT: PRINCIPLES & PRACTICES
Second Edition
Edited by Greg Denton, Lori E. Raleigh, and A. J. Singh

MANAGING BEVERAGE OPERATIONS
Second Edition
Ronald F. Cichy/Lendal H. Kotschevar

FOOD SAFETY: MANAGING WITH THE HACCP SYSTEM
Second Edition
Ronald F. Cichy

UNIFORM SYSTEM OF FINANCIAL REPORTING FOR SPAS

FUNDAMENTALS OF DESTINATION MANAGEMENT AND MARKETING
Edited by Rich Harrill

ETHICS IN THE HOSPITALITY AND TOURISM INDUSTRY
Second Edition
Karen Lieberman/Bruce Nissen

HOSPITALITY AND TOURISM MARKETING
William Lazer/Melissa Dallas/Carl Riegel

SPA: A COMPREHENSIVE INTRODUCTION
Elizabeth M. Johnson/Bridgette M. Redman

HOSPITALITY 2015: THE FUTURE OF HOSPITALITY AND TRAVEL
Marvin Cetron/Fred DeMicco/Owen Davies

REVENUE MANAGEMENT: MAXIMIZING REVENUE IN HOSPITALITY OPERATIONS
Gabor Forgacs

REVENUE MANAGEMENT

Maximizing Revenue in Hospitality Operations

Gabor Forgacs, Dr. oec.

Disclaimer

This publication is designed to provide accurate and authoritative information in regard to the subject matter covered. It is sold with the understanding that the publisher is not engaged in rendering legal, accounting, or other professional service. If legal advice or other expert assistance is required, the services of a competent professional person should be sought.

—*From the Declaration of Principles jointly adopted by the American Bar Association and a Committee of Publishers and Associations*

The author, Gabor Forgacs, is solely responsible for the contents of this publication. All views expressed herein are solely those of the author and do not necessarily reflect the views of the American Hotel & Lodging Educational Institute (the Institute) or the American Hotel & Lodging Association (AH&LA).

Nothing contained in this publication shall constitute a standard, an endorsement, or a recommendation of the Institute or AH&LA. The Educational Institute and AH&LA disclaim any liability with respect to the use of any information, procedure, or product, or reliance thereon by any member of the hospitality industry.

2113 N. High Street
Lansing, Michigan 48906-4221

The American Hotel & Lodging
Educational Institute is a nonprofit
educational foundation.

Printed in the United States of America
3 4 5 6 7 8 9 10 13 12 11 10

ISBN: 978-0-86612-348-8

Editor: Timothy J. Eaton

Contents

Foreword

There could not be a better time to introduce a comprehensive book on revenue management into educational institutions and the hospitality industry as a whole. As a discipline, this vital area of expertise has advanced almost beyond recognition when compared to the comparatively basic tactics employed in the 1980s and early 1990s. From forecasting to distribution, from a focus on largely tactical issues to highly strategic decision-making—revenue management has evolved into a unique and critically important part of hotel profit optimization.

This trend toward a separate and specialized discipline has been spurred on by the convergence of a number of factors. In the past decade, hospitality as an industry has undergone not one but two "perfect storms."

We experienced the first perfect storm when significant economic pressure coincided with the strong emergence of the Internet, which in turn overlapped the events of 9/11. When the "tech bubble" burst, a significant downturn in the economy ensued. Although the technology sector represented just one factor in the economic decline, there was also growing pressure from Wall Street on publicly owned hotel companies to meet profit expectations. Quickly, day-to-day hotel operators found themselves not in the hotel business but in the business of hotels.

Then came 9/11—a tragic event that had a devastating effect on the industry—and the result was "every man for himself." Enter the Internet in a very big way, and the way we did business was changed forever. All of a sudden, long-held pricing secrets became public knowledge, transparent for any consumer to see. Rate wars and insane discounting led to the commoditization of room inventory. It became evident very quickly that, as an industry, our knowledge of a key element of revenue management—strategic pricing—was severely lacking. The mantra of the day was price parity at all costs—a pathetically short-sighted answer to pricing integrity issues.

We were forced by these colliding events to do a much better job of practicing revenue management. No longer was it sufficient to carry out tactical revenue management decisions as part of some other function, such as reservations. The stand-alone position of "revenue manager" and/or "director of revenue management" became both a reality and a necessity. The teaching of revenue management as a discipline and the emergence of certifications in revenue management are just two examples of the rapid evolution of this specialized area of the industry.

Yet as the discipline evolves, we are facing a second, perhaps even more powerful "perfect storm." In just the last few years there has been an incredible convergence of technology, demographics, and global economic factors that have created (as Don Tapscott, a Wikinomics contributor, suggests) a Category 6 storm in the evolution of traditional business models. I'm referring to the impact of Web 2.0, or what some are referring to as "weapons of mass collaboration."

Out of this storm, Travel 2.0 is emerging. Supplier-controlled, static content is giving way to consumer-controlled, dynamic content. For example, gone are the days when a hotel could focus solely on traditional competitive benchmarking. Today, consumer-generated media (CGM) is an even more important gauge of competitive positioning than a market share report. And recent research indicates that as much as 80 percent of all travel decisions are made or influenced online—even if the actual reservation is not booked electronically.

Couple Travel 2.0 trends with advances in technology (billions of mobile electronic devices have been shipped in the past several years, for example) and changing demographics (recent studies indicate that more than 50 percent of all teenagers between the ages of 12 and 17 are content creators), and you can see why we are being compelled to learn our business all over again.

Now we're witnessing a unique, unprecedented interdependence of disciplines. Demand creation (marketing), demand capture (sales), and demand management (revenue management) are all converging in ways that make the director of revenue the key person in the new business model. The need to practice total revenue management (the optimization of all revenue streams) in a far more sophisticated manner than previously required is now mandatory. Today, revenue management expertise is not "nice-to-have" but "need-to-have."

How does all of this relate to a book about the discipline of revenue management? There is not a single element of revenue management that isn't affected by these events. Whether it's competitive benchmarking and strategic pricing, or demand forecasting and distribution management, the need for better education and more sophisticated revenue management practices is essential to the survival of the industry. Gabor Forgacs, a leading educator, has taken the time and energy to write a comprehensive overview of this discipline as it is today. Recognizing that revenue management is indeed a distinct discipline with the need for very specialized education is a vital step in continuing to move the discipline forward, even as consumer buying behavior speeds through change after change.

Bonnie E. Buckhiester
International Society of Hospitality Consultants

Bonnie Buckhiester is the President and CEO of Buckhiester Management, the leading revenue management consulting firm in North America, and a member of the board of directors of the International Society of Hospitality Consultants.

Preface

As a general manager of a small full-service property, I dreamed about hiring capable and willing maintenance staff, such as an electrician who could not only replace the cylinder of a guestroom door lock but, if push came to shove, would not shy away from unplugging a clogged guestroom toilet. As the manager ultimately responsible for everything, I had to juggle many duties and responsibilities myself, from negotiating with asphalt companies to repave our parking lot, to discussing the hotel's room upgrade policies with a loyal guest, to dealing with an unpleasant manager of a travel agency who called to complain about the menu choices at our hotel and the water temperature of our swimming pool. All of this was attended to while I wrote a report to the local fire marshal regarding the hotel's battery-renewal policies and procedures for our smoke sensors. And this was just one average morning of one average day at the hotel. So many hats to wear, so many disciplines to master—never a dull moment! The hotel business is interdisciplinary, just as life is. No wonder that the newest emerging discipline in the hotel industry, called revenue management, is also interdisciplinary in its nature. Revenue management can add new dimensions of strategic thinking and become a value-added enabler of sustainable corporate growth in the highly competitive hospitality field.

Practicing sound revenue management strategies and tactics affects almost everything a hotel does. Revenue management involves all facets of operations management—room rates, demand forecasting, and customer relations management, among many other areas. Marketing, accounting, operations management, and finances are all involved in devising revenue management strategies. Hoteliers involved in every aspect of their hotels' operations will comfortably navigate this book. Those hotel managers and employees who work for large properties and whose responsibilities are narrowed down to one particular hotel division may use this book to broaden their horizons. Hospitality students who have mastered at least introductory-level marketing, accounting, and front office management courses can build on that knowledge by reading this book. All future owners and managers of hotels will discover a discipline that will help their hotels become more profitable.

Acknowledgments

I would like to take this opportunity to express my gratitude to those who have provided help and support along the way. I was fortunate to enjoy a full-year sabbatical from my teaching duties at Ryerson University, and I feel truly blessed for this opportunity provided by my employer.

I have learned much—and keep learning!—from all of my students, both at the undergraduate level at the Ted Rogers School of Management at Ryerson University and also from my MBA students at the University of Guelph.

Authors need the constructive criticism and guidance of others to gain insight and inspiration, and I have received valuable help from many people, too numerous to list. However, this book would not have been completed without the important contributions of some key individuals that I must acknowledge. My special thanks goes out to Bonnie Buckhiester of Buckhiester Management for her continued support of my work, and to Scott Farrell of TravelCLICK for his invaluable feedback and help. I also must thank my colleague, Professor Bernie McEvoy, who provided much encouragement and input.

I hope this book on revenue management will be followed by many others from a variety of authors, in order to build a solid theoretical foundation for this exciting new discipline—a discipline that has the potential to change the hotel industry for the better.

Dr. Gabor Forgacs
Toronto, Ontario
Canada

About the Author

GABOR FORGACS has twenty years' work experience in the hotel industry on two continents, including a management position at a Four Seasons hotel in Toronto, Ontario, Canada, and the position of president and general manager of a full-service hotel in Budapest, Hungary. Since 1997 he has taught at the Ted Rogers School of Hospitality and Tourism Management at Ryerson University in Toronto. He teaches courses in "Revenue Management for Hospitality & Tourism," "The Value of Branding in Lodging," and "Property Management Systems." Dr. Forgacs is also a member of the Special Graduate Faculty of the School of Hospitality & Tourism Management at the University of Guelph, Ontario, Canada, where he teaches advanced revenue management for the MBA program. He received his doctorate from the Budapest University of Economic Sciences. He also holds an undergraduate degree in economics from the same university, and he is a graduate of the College of Commerce and Hotel Management of Budapest, Hungary.

Dr. Forgacs is the editor of the online discussion series "Branding and Product Specialization in Hotels" sponsored by Henry Stewart Publications (2009), and he was invited to participate as a content expert in the development of training and educational materials on revenue management by the American Hotel & Lodging Educational Institute (2000).

Dr. Forgacs has published articles in the *International Journal of Contemporary Hospitality Management, The Hotelier Magazine* (Canada), *The Rooms Chronicle* (United States), *The Accommodator* (Canada), the *Canadian Lodging News*, and other print magazines. He has been published in the conference proceedings of ICHRIE (International Council on Hotel, Restaurant and Institutional Education), and has published material online for Hotel-Online.com, ehotelier.com, hotel-newsresource.com, 4hoteliers.com, htrends.com, HVS International.com, and other websites. Dr. Forgacs is frequently quoted and interviewed in the Canadian media regarding revenue management and other hospitality issues.

Chapter 1 Outline

A Brief History
Criteria for Effective Use
  Fixed-Capacity Environment
  Perishable Products
  Varied but Predictable Demand
  High Fixed Costs and Low Variable Costs

Competencies

1. Define revenue management and identify the basic steps of the revenue management process. (p. 3)
2. Outline the brief history of revenue management and why it has become important. (pp. 3–6)
3. Identify and describe the business traits that allow for the best use of revenue management. (pp. 6–10)

1

What Is Revenue Management?

REVENUE MANAGEMENT, sometimes called yield management, has become part of mainstream business theory and practice over the last fifteen to twenty years. Whether we call it an emerging discipline or a new management science—it has been called both—revenue management is a set of revenue maximization strategies and tactics meant to improve the profitability of certain businesses. It is complex because it involves several aspects of management control, including rate management, revenue streams management, and distribution channel management, just to name a few. Revenue management is multidisciplinary because it blends elements of marketing, operations, and financial management into a highly successful new approach. A revenue manager frequently must work with one or more other departments when designing and implementing revenue management strategies.

Quite a few managers tend to look at revenue management from a narrow perspective, seeing it as only a push-pull game with rates. Revenue management involves much more than just crunching numbers and adjusting price points. It encompasses product definition, competitive benchmarking, strategic pricing, demand forecasting, business mix manipulation, and distribution channel management (see Exhibit 1). The process is a dynamic and perpetual business cycle that requires all the components to be aligned and seamlessly integrated to ensure full functionality. In hotels, revenue management is used to examine how many room nights are sold (occupancy), at what rate (discounting), what else is sold (sales mix), to whom (market segmentation), and through what channel (distribution channel management). All these are examined and managed with the objective of optimizing income under constantly changing supply and demand conditions.

Before we begin applying revenue management to hospitality operations, however, let's look briefly at how we got here.

A Brief History

Revenue management is a relatively new discipline that grew out of the airline industry's yield management initiatives of the mid-1980s. Following the deregulation of the U.S. airline industry in 1978, drastic changes took effect. Low-cost suppliers appeared that aggressively carved out a growing share of the market. The legacy carriers had a hard time figuring out how to compete successfully with the charters and the discount airlines. By the mid-1980s, the threat became serious.

Exhibit 1 Revenue Management as a Business Process

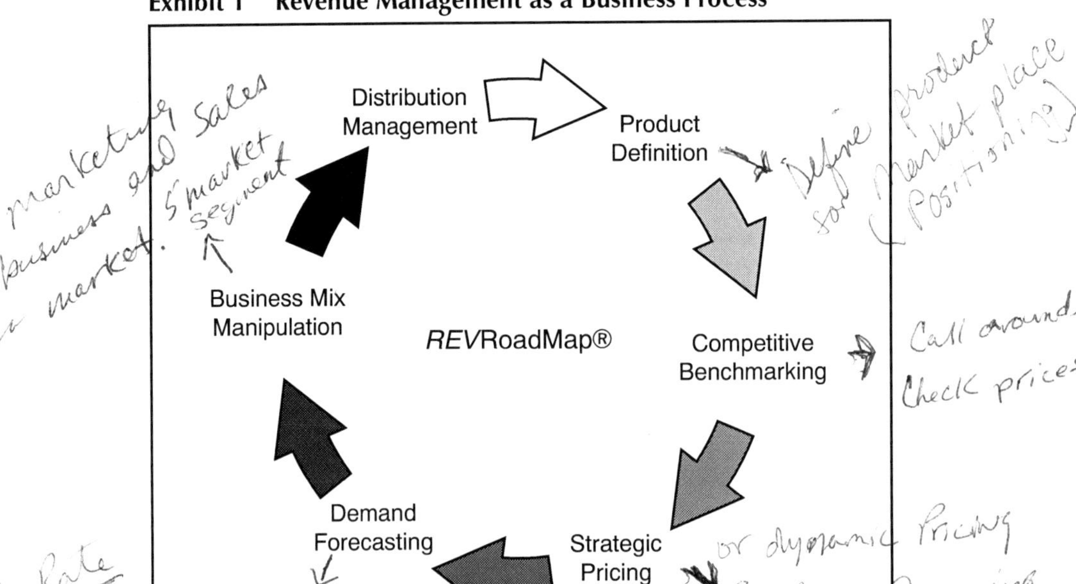

Robert L. Crandall, the legendary chairman and CEO of American Airlines, fronted a new approach to tackle the problem: he used yield management to manipulate seat inventories by different fare classes on each flight. Discount allocations were based on solid data, and computers (mainframe systems at the time) were used to process massive amounts of information to deal with constantly changing market demand and competitive fares from other airlines. Forecasting became crucial. Following the successful implementation of yield management, multi-tiered rate structures (coupled with forecasting accuracy and market segmentation) became the focus of strategic thinking.

A number of industries realized their business models were similar to that of the airlines in terms of product perishability, seasonality of demand, and cost structure: hotels, cruise lines, car rental agencies, broadcasters, and the entertainment industry were among the first to embrace revenue management. Tactics to increase occupancy were used in low-demand periods, and premium pricing was used to improve income generation in high-demand periods. The financial rewards were measurable in revenue performance and increased profit.

The biggest chains traditionally take the lead on new initiatives in the hotel industry. Central reservation systems, franchising, and management contracts illustrate this, as do no-smoking floors, interactive television for in-room entertainment, and Internet access. Big brands were also at the forefront when it came to implementing revenue management systems. Some companies developed proprietary systems, while others elected to purchase a system from a supplier. Quite a few corporations were content with a spreadsheet-based tool developed by their

Yield Management or Revenue Management?

There is no difference between yield management and revenue management in the context of the hotel industry. The only reason the term "yield management" is still frequently used is that it was the commonly accepted term in the early years because of its airline industry origins.

Initially, the European (mostly British) revenue management literature had also a preference for the term "yield management," while the North American literature had a preference for the term "revenue management." Today it is fair to say that there is no substantial difference between the meanings of these terms and the prevailing industry jargon has leaned toward accepting the use of "revenue management" in the context of the hotel business.

Revenue management is a discipline that enables hotels to become more profitable. In order to achieve measurable outcomes, carefully selected strategies and tactics are deployed based on an analysis of supply/demand dynamics and a given hotel's products' attributes. The most successful hotels know exactly what their core competencies are, who their guests are, how to market to them, and what it takes to meet or exceed their expectations. They also control their expenses, but most importantly, they understand that the key of sustainable success in this industry is in revenue generation. Occupancy alone is not enough. Average rate alone is not enough. Today's managers need to drive both.

own front office and reservations people. Most tactical-level measures of revenue management can be sufficiently controlled with a simple spreadsheet designed by those who use it every day.

Today, most hotels use revenue management in one way or another. The level of automation and the degree of sophistication vary, but most hotels in competitive markets use multi-tiered rate structures that they can adjust based on key variables. The strategic understanding may differ from brand to brand, but most hotels use a variety of channels to sell their room inventory, and they are knowledgeable users of revenue management tactics at the front office level.

The hotel industry now recognizes revenue management as one of the core competencies vital to profitability. However, not everything done in the name of revenue management is new. Some revenue management tactics are as old as the industrial age. When railways gave people the ability to travel in masses, a new lodging industry started to grow. Hotels were built to accommodate travelers at frequented locations. Those who managed hotels as a profession embraced good business sense from early on. They learned the difference between seasons of high and low demand. They recognized that the selling price for one room sold to one guest needed to be different from the selling price for dozens of rooms sold to the same guest. They could distinguish the guest who spent money only on the room from others who spent much more on food, drink, and other services. Hoteliers always recognized return guests and appreciated their patronage. Hotel managers greeted those arrivals personally, offered upgrades, and devoted heightened attention to them.

Although the world has changed a lot, the hospitality industry's core concept of providing accommodation for a fee has remained unchanged. The terminology may be different today, but seasonal prices, packages, volume discounts, loyalty, and average spending per stay are not new concepts at all. Hoteliers like Cesar Ritz, Ellsworth Statler, and William Waldorf Astor conducted their business using manual systems based on paper and pencil. Service was second to none and good hotels made decent profits. So, is there anything new under the sun?

Actually, yes. While many tasks now done under the name of revenue management have been done since the nineteenth century, technology has greatly increased the complexity of the information that can be analyzed and the speed at which it can be done. Furthermore, the hotel industry is not the same as it was a hundred years ago. It has become a global industry. The complex expectations placed on today's managers far surpass the expectations of a century ago. Financial pressures have changed significantly since the trend of separating ownership and management became prevalent for midsize and larger properties in the last quarter of the twentieth century in North America.

On the supply side, the markets became much more fragmented and competitive. On the demand side, travelers have more clout than ever, largely because they have information on virtually everything at their fingertips. Today's travelers routinely comparison shop. On the operational side, it is not just room service or the front desk that is expected to work at all hours. Guests expect to be able to access hotel room availability information whenever they want it. They want to make or change reservations and make payments around the clock as well. Time has become a new currency. Guests demand that their wants and needs be met immediately. These expectations dictate a dynamic operational environment from service providers, where both people and systems must be able to handle a lot of tasks accurately and efficiently.

Criteria for Effective Use

Many businesses use some revenue management elements. For example, various businesses use forecasting and seasonal pricing changes and have learned how their clientele can be segmented into clusters based on buying behavior. However, a business or industry needs to meet specific criteria in order to unlock the full potential of revenue management. Businesses that benefit the most from revenue management:

1. Work in fixed capacity environments.
2. Have perishable or time-sensitive products.
3. Face varied but predictable demand over time.
4. Have a high proportion of fixed costs and a low proportion of variable costs.

Hospitality is one of these businesses. Let's look at these criteria more fully.

Fixed-Capacity Environment

Some businesses face few constraints on their potential sales. They can meet higher demand by producing more units. If we sell books and the market wants more, we

> **110 Percent Occupancy?**
>
> Under certain conditions, hotels may seem to defy the laws of mathematics by logging occupancies of greater than 100 percent. How is this possible? First, it can only happen in a sellers' market. East European countries in the 1970s make a good illustration. There was a serious shortage in room supply at a time when incoming tourism started to grow. It became a sellers' market fast. Second, most of the tourists arrived in tour groups. The Hotel National, a city center hotel in Budapest, Hungary, was a typical case. Every night, the hotel was filled up to capacity with groups, most of them one-night stays. During the day, the hotel was also a popular place for locals who needed a day-use room only in the afternoon hours. The hotel rented out rooms for the day-use guests in the afternoon, then had the rooms cleaned and turned over for the groups checking in after dinner. Group contracts typically allowed a 10 percent tolerance. This meant that that if the reserved room block was for twenty rooms, the invoice could be made out for eighteen rooms even if the group actually needed only seventeen or fewer rooms on arrival. In other words, the same room might be sold for day use, charged to a group account despite remaining unused, and sold to an actual user all on the same day. This was not unusual during those years, and it sometimes resulted in annual average occupancies of greater than 100 percent in the second half of the 1970s. Those days are long gone.

can increase output as needed. On the other hand, if demand drops, we can lower the amount we print, decrease inventory, shorten the hours of operation, and wait until demand strengthens.

Businesses with fixed capacity do not have these options. Fixed capacity is a significant constraint. Hotels have a finite number of hotel rooms to sell. They can't sell more than their total capacity even when the demand is there. The same capacity exists when demand is low.

Actually, given sufficient time, even fixed capacity can be changed or rearranged. Some sources use the term *relatively fixed* for this reason. We can't change the number of rooms in a hotel overnight. However, if we see a permanent need for more units, we can always consider adding a new wing or another floor. But it takes months or years to do it. We can't address short-term demand fluctuations with capacity changes.

A restaurant may open a patio, change its service style, or reconfigure its table mix to loosen its capacity constraints, but these measures also have limitations. Production capacity constraints will limit the number of guests a restaurant can serve in a meal period. Fire safety regulations often limit the number of persons allowed on the premises at any given time.

Perishable Products

A hotel sells a time-sensitive product—the privilege to occupy a given room for a given time. After the time expires, the hotel has the opportunity to clean, refresh, and replenish the room and sell the privilege of staying there again to another occupant.

Tonight's room night has a short shelf life. Tonight's room night cannot be sold tomorrow. If a hotel can't sell a room night and a room remains unsold, the hotel can't store that unsold room in inventory and sell it later. Tomorrow, the hotel will sell tomorrow's room night.

Businesses that sell tangible, non-perishable products may use their inventory as a buffer. Unsold units can be inventoried. What they haven't sold one day, they may sell the following day. Hotels, airlines, cruise ships, and theaters deal in perishable products. Unsold room nights, plane seats, state rooms, and tickets can't be sold the next day. These products are called perishable to reflect this special attribute. As a consequence of this fundamental trait, the pressure to close a sale is significant. Lost opportunities have a strong negative impact on profitability.

Varied but Predictable Demand

In the hotel industry, demand fluctuates all the time. There are differences between geographical markets and property types, but virtually all hotels face some sort of seasonal demand variances. A warm winter resort hotel on a Caribbean island will have different seasonal demand fluctuations than a transient hotel in Paris, but both can identify their own main seasons, off-seasons, and shoulder seasons.

Seasonality refers to a variation of demand based on the season of the year. But demand fluctuations can be observed by days of the week as well. Saturday was the highest occupancy day in North American hotels for many years. Demand fluctuations have operational consequences: busy days and slow days dictate different rhythms in the life of a hotel. Changes can be observed even within a day: the morning rush, the midday lull, and the evening rush are characteristic of a transient hotel's life. Traffic patterns in a casino hotel differ from those in a spa hotel. Again, each hotel can describe its own seasonality within a year, a week, or a day.

Varying demand helps to put revenue management into perspective: the impacts or measures of revenue management in a hotel cannot be perceived like they would be in a static environment. The approach to revenue management is based on the understanding that everything is in permanent flux. For example, the number of reservations on the books seven days out will likely be different from the number on the books for that same day only three days out. Guests cancel or modify their reservations and new guests book at the last minute. Hotels do not provide a static operational environment.

Does this ever-changing operating environment create chaotic nightmares for management? Not at all, as the fluctuations show certain patterns. This is where the concept of predictability becomes fundamental. The beginnings and endings of seasons can be identified. A hotel's records document the rush hours and the high-occupancy days and weeks. The revenue impact of statutory holidays, school breaks, and significant events in the hotel's vicinity can be predicted. This knowledge can be used to prepare demand forecasts. Accurate forecasts allow management to use appropriate pricing, product packaging (bundling), and other strategies more effectively.

One of the challenges for management is finding the right tactics based on the right strategy to arrive at optimal solutions in a constantly changing environment. Revenue management can work with valuable data to identify and map out the seasonality of demand. Identifiable revenue patterns will help determine best-suited strategies and tactics to exploit revenue maximization opportunities.

High Fixed Costs and Low Variable Costs

Some expense items are not affected by occupancy. If a cost is not directly related to sales volume, it can be classified as fixed cost. For example, mortgage payments, insurance premiums, amortization of capital assets, the payroll costs of annual salaries, energy, and maintenance are all fixed-cost items.

Some people question whether salaried payroll and energy costs should be seen as fixed items. But, according to property management literature, more than 80 percent of a hotel's energy cost depends on weather conditions rather than occupancy levels. Hot and humid days require a lot of air conditioning; cold days with strong windchill factors require a lot of heating. Hotels cannot necessarily seal off unoccupied rooms or floors. In that sense, most of the energy and maintenance costs are fairly considered fixed items, as they do not directly depend on sales and occupancy performance.

The only portion of the payroll that can be directly related to occupancy and sales is seasonal labor, part-time employees' wages, and the overtime cost of hourly workers. Therefore, most of a hotel's labor cost also can be considered fixed costs.

It is important to note that the fixed costs are also the big-ticket ones. They make up most of the total costs of operation. This cost structure reflects the fact that the hotel industry is capital-intensive. It takes a significant initial investment to secure a piece of land, build a hotel on it, and furnish it with all the necessary fixtures, furniture, and equipment. Once the place is ready to open, the operational costs will have to include a lot of fixed items as a result of all the required capital and resources tied up in those assets. As a real estate property, a hotel needs to carry those fixed costs, which are not reflective of the hotel's daily operating performance.

Hotels are not just capital assets, but also income-generating businesses. All those cost items that are directly related to selling a unit (room night) are classified as variable. There is no need to clean and re-supply a room if it remains vacant one night. Variable costs can also be described as the cost differential between an occupied and a vacant room.

The variable cost of a room night is the dollar amount it would cost on average to make up one room and get it ready for new occupancy. The steps involved in changing a room status from *occupied* to *vacant* varies based on the level of service and amenities a hotel provides. Cleaning and providing fresh linen, towels, and bathroom supplies are always part of the costs, as is the housekeeper's wages for the time spent on the room. High-end hotels may offer more gadgets, but they have to meet higher expectations as well. Even if a hotel does not offer designer bathrobes, the highest thread-count sheets, chocolate truffles, and remote controlled shades, the basics that are provided to each new arriving guest can cost the hotelier $10 to $40 per day. An unsold room does not incur this charge.

Revenue maximization is the logical way to address profitability challenges in the hotel business. Hotels need to drive top-line revenue to cover expenses and allow for profit. Cutting costs is seldom as effective, not only because it tends to harm the quality of service, but also because the only costs a hotel can manipulate in the short term are the variable ones, which constitute a small portion of total costs. The only way to achieve sustainable financial success is by maximizing top-line revenue. The bottom line will be favorable only if the top line is strong and steady enough to meet financial objectives. Revenue management is critically important in meeting this challenge.

Chapter 2 Outline

Competencies

1. Identify, define, and calculate several important internal performance measures that help to evaluate the results of operation. (pp. 13–23)
2. Describe the purpose of a competitive set and the factors one must consider when creating one properly. (pp. 23–27)
3. Calculate market share and penetration indexes and explain what they reveal. (pp. 27–30)
4. Identify potential sources of market intelligence. (pp. 30–31)
5. Discuss the significant challenges that beset most forms of measurement and the efforts to interpret measurement results. (pp. 31–32)

2

Measurement

IN ORDER TO MANAGE A BUSINESS EFFECTIVELY, one generally must have quantifiable goals and the means to measure how well those goals are being attained. There are both internal and external measures or standards against which managers can evaluate the results of operations. The most useful internal measures will relate to the primary products and services a business provides. In the lodging industry, the primary product is the room night. As might be expected, most internal performance measures relate to the sales of room nights and the revenue generated from those sales. Important external measures look at the business in the context of the overall market and in relation to the business's competition.

This chapter looks at a number of the most important internal and external measures used in managing a hotel or other lodging operation.

Internal Measures

While revenue management is more than crunching numbers, the proper calculation of the most meaningful performance indicators is imperative. Management must be able to measure performance accurately. Hotels are capital-intensive businesses, and investors expect to be rewarded for their investments and the risks those investments entail. Investors will seek other investment options if a hotel's financial rewards are not aligned with their expectations. If other local properties, hotels in other markets, or other commercial real estate businesses provide better returns under substantially equal risk, investors may divest their interests in underperforming hotel assets and pursue their options elsewhere. The industry has witnessed such actions many times under such labels as "divestment of non-core assets," "diversification of investment portfolios," or "strategic re-alignment of the asset base," among others. If the asset performs up to expectations, everything looks fine. Once an asset can't produce the expected return, the weighing of options begins. Revenue management can improve financial performance, thereby making the property a more attractive option for some investors. Conversely, some investors frequently seek to acquire underperforming assets and turn them around by introducing revenue maximization strategies.

The only way to determine whether a hotel is underperforming is to measure the hotel's performance in comparison with some standard. Measurements are of little use without context. If a hotel has 70 percent occupancy in June, how does management decide whether this is good or bad? Internal performance measures are most commonly compared with three general standards. One standard is historical figures from comparable earlier periods. The past records of operation are crucial to have as a starting point of reference. If the above hotel has had 80 percent occupancies in the previous two Junes, the 70 percent figure for this June may be problematic. But if the hotel's previous years' figures for June were 50 and 60 percent, respectively, this year's figure has quite a different meaning.

The second common standard is the budget. If the hotel has budgeted for June with an expectation of 85 percent occupancy, an actual occupancy of 70 percent will likely call for investigation into the causes of the shortfall. The third common standard is industry averages. When using industry averages, be careful to include only properties comparable in size, amenities, level of service, market orientation, age, and geographic market, if possible. Overall industry averages will include many kinds of properties that have little in common with any particular property, so those numbers will often reveal little of real use. But industry averages of comparable properties will provide an idea of how one property's performance compares with its industry segment.

New hotel developments have no historic data. In these cases, comparable hotels must be looked at and used as points of reference. There are excellent sources of information where data of this nature can be purchased.[1] These third-party sources frequently will also provide an analysis of whether the numbers need adjustment for a specific property.

When a hotel wants to improve its profitability, the first set of data to consider is the hotel's historic data. As stated earlier, the most informative variables will be based on the hotel's product—the room night. Historical unit sales and revenue generated provide the first data set to look into.

Revenue

Revenue is the amount of sales, measured in the appropriate currency, generated from the sale of goods and services. The annual income statement has an entry for revenue for a business. It is customary to refer to revenue as a *top-line* item to reflect its position in the income statement (see Exhibit 1). This number can be broken down into quarterly, monthly, weekly, or even daily numbers if that helps our analysis. The sales revenue data must be kept on file as it is generated, and it should be accessible any time management needs it. It can be compared as current year over last year, actual vs. budget, the fiscal year-to-date, or any other way that serves a purpose.

Revenue can also be broken down by revenue centers. Room revenue is particularly important for revenue management and will be the first focus. Once managers have a good handle on room revenue management and implement revenue maximization strategies, they should move on and broaden the scope to total revenue management involving all the other revenue streams as well. These other revenue streams may include food and beverage, catering, function space rental, spa, parking, retail sales, and other revenues depending on the particulars of a given operation.

The formula for determining room revenue is quite straightforward:

$$\text{Room revenue} = \text{Room nights sold} \times \text{Room rate charged}$$

For example, if a hotel sells 6,450 room nights at \$122 per room, room revenue will equal 6,450 × \$122, or \$786,900.

Exhibit 1 Income Statement Format

STATEMENT OF INCOME

	Period	
	Current Year	**Prior Year**
REVENUE		
Rooms	$	$
Food and Beverage		
Other Operated Departments		
Rentals and Other Income		
Total Revenue		
EXPENSES		
Rooms		
Food and Beverage		
Other Operated Departments		
Administrative and General		
Sales and Marketing		
Property Operation and Maintenance		
Utilities		
Management Fees		
Rent, Property Taxes, and Insurance		
Interest Expense		
Depreciation and Amortization		
Loss or (Gain) on the Disposition of Assets		
Total Expenses		
INCOME BEFORE INCOME TAXES		
INCOME TAXES		
Current		
Deferred		
Total Income Taxes		
NET INCOME	$	$

Source: *Uniform System of Accounts for the Lodging Industry,* Tenth Revised Edition (Lansing, Mich.: American Hotel & Lodging Educational Institute, 2006), p. 18.

Occupancy Percentage

Occupancy percentage is one of the most common performance measures in the lodging industry. It expresses the proportion of rooms sold to total rooms. The formula is:

$$\text{Occupancy percentage} = \frac{\text{Room nights sold in a period}}{\text{Room nights available in that same period}} \times 100$$

For example, consider a 300-unit hotel that has sold 1,428 room nights in one week. Total room nights available will equal 300 rooms × 7 nights, or 2,100 room nights. The weekly occupancy of the hotel is therefore 1,428 ÷ 2,100 × 100, or 68 percent.

Neither occupancy percentage nor revenue should be analyzed on their own. Both need to be considered when we examine a hotel's performance.

Average Daily Rate

The *average daily rate (ADR)* expresses the average room rate realized from the sale of rooms in a given period. It should be calculated on a daily, weekly, and monthly basis. The formula is:

$$\text{ADR} = \frac{\text{Room revenue}}{\text{Number of room nights sold}}$$

For example, if total room revenue for a week is $114,240 and the hotel sold 1,428 room nights that week, the ADR is $114,240 ÷ 1,428, or $80.

Tracking and benchmarking the ADR is important. A hotel makes an effort to charge rates that both provide the perception of value for the guest and allow the hotel to realize its financial objectives. The traditional expectation of ADR is that it will gradually increase from year to year. However, circumstances may at times thwart that expectation. Market pressures or the aging of a property may cause an ADR to fall from one fiscal period to another. Calculating and tracking ADR changes allows management to quantify the impact of price changes, get closer to their root causes, and see what can be done about the problem. In some cases, a declining ADR is caused by an inferior product. If management chooses not to invest in an upgrade, the hotel can keep losing market share. When reinvestment is not chosen or available, such hotels are sometimes significantly repositioned down-market; for example, a struggling upper-tier hotel might be successfully repositioned as a competitive mid-tier hotel after reflagging the property.

The question of whether complimentary room nights should be included in the ADR calculation sometimes comes up. According to the *Uniform System of Accounts for the Lodging Industry,* they should not. Those room nights were not sold and did not generate room revenue, so including them would distort the result of an ADR calculation. If a room night was not sold for revenue, it should not be counted for sales performance analysis.

RevPAR

Occupancy percentage and ADR are both common performance measures, but sometimes they can appear to disagree. Consider a hotel on two nights. The first night, the hotel has 70 percent occupancy with an ADR of $95. The second night, the hotel has 75 percent occupancy with an ADR of $90. Which appears to be the better situation? ADR suggests the first night, but occupancy percentage suggests the second night. One way to resolve this conflict is to combine occupancy percentage and ADR into a single statistic. This combined measure is called *revenue per available room (RevPAR).* RevPAR is a way of evaluating management's success in realizing the business potential of a hotel in a given period. RevPAR calculations have become popular in recent years as the most frequently used measure of room revenue performance. There are two formulas for calculating RevPAR:

$$\text{RevPAR} = \frac{\text{Room revenue for a period}}{\text{Total rooms available for that period}}$$

$$\text{RevPAR} = \text{ADR} \times \text{Occupancy percentage}$$

The two formulas produce the same result.

In the example above, the RevPAR for the first night is $95 × 70%, or $66.50. The RevPAR for the second night is $90 × 75%, or $67.50. From a revenue or RevPAR standpoint, the second night appears to be preferable.

RevPAR can be a useful performance indicator, but users must be careful not to read more into it than is there. First, RevPAR inherently appears to favor the result that produces the highest revenue. But it will not always be true that the highest revenue also produces the highest profit. RevPAR ignores cost factors that must also be considered. Second, and more interesting from a revenue management view, similar or even identical RevPARs may result from very different operating positions. Consider two scenarios in a 120-unit hotel. In the first scenario, the hotel sells 66 room nights at an ADR of $100. In the second scenario, the hotel sells 100 room nights at an ADR of $66. In both situations, total room revenue is $6,600 and RevPAR is $55. Are these scenarios equivalent? In terms of room revenue, yes. But the total revenue earned comes from very different operating circumstances. Is one preferable? How might a preference be determined?

Before we address those questions, consider what might drive the hotel—intentionally or not—toward one result over the other. It is a management truism that a business will get the employee behavior it rewards. If the reward system is not properly aligned with management's goals, the chance of reaching those goals is diminished. If the reward system favors higher ADRs, the front office manager's incentive will be to drive ADR, resulting in a preference for the first scenario ($100 ADR). If the reward system rewards the front office manager for filling rooms, the manager will prefer and work toward the higher occupancy percentage (83.33 percent) of the second scenario. If the reward system favors RevPAR, a manager might see the two scenarios as essentially equivalent.

So, is one scenario more desirable? The answer is almost certainly yes, but *which one* is preferable will vary by hotel. There is no easy way to choose one scenario over the other because there are arguments for and against both. The argument for selling at a higher ADR with a lower occupancy is that the hotel will have fewer rooms to clean for the same revenue, so variable costs will be minimized. The argument for higher occupancy at a lower ADR is that having more guests could lead to additional revenue opportunities in the hotel's other revenue centers (parking, food and beverage, pay-per-view movie sales, etc.). Until we determine and compare the variable cost savings of the first scenario with the expected additional net revenue of the second scenario, we cannot identify the better option.

For that matter, even *after* we perform such a comparison, the answer may remain unresolved. This is because, despite their equivalent revenues, a revenue manager would see the two scenarios as being significantly different and the results of very different strategies. A guest willing to pay $100 for a room night is neither better nor worse than a guest willing to pay $66 per room night for the same room. But it needs to be recognized that these two guests belong to different market segments and targeting them requires distinctly different approaches. A hotel needs to identify its prime target market. Because a lot of other decisions flow from this market choice, the choice to be in the $66 ADR market or the $100 ADR market is a strategic decision.

In other words, a high ADR is not inherently better than a low ADR. The *appropriateness* of the ADR for the given hotel and target market is the central issue. Mid-market hotels might provide better profitability than luxury hotels in certain markets. The two hotel types require different investments per room and have different operational costs, staffing levels, clienteles, and revenue mixes to start with. The popularity of limited-service hotels (those offering no food service outlets) is proof that there are lucrative returns in strategic decisions to enter carefully chosen markets with the right product, regardless of price points. It would be a tremendous mistake to believe that only glamorous high-end hotels make good businesses. ADR alone is in no way indicative of financial success or failure. The answer to the question of whether the $66 or $100 ADR is preferred is ultimately this: it depends on the business strategy of the given hotel.

As is true with all performance measures, it is important that management track RevPAR over a period of time so that significant changes can be identified and, if necessary, investigated. A change in RevPAR can be the result of a change in either ADR or occupancy, but in real life it is unusual to have the luxury of simple scenarios. Most likely, changes tend to happen in both. Revenue managers have to look beyond the figures to see the underlying trends in order to evaluate and make strategic decisions. The revenue manager's analysis should identify which component (ADR or occupancy) is the primary driver of the change. Suppose analysis reveals that an increase in ADR was driven by rate increases rather than occupancy. Some issues to consider would then be: How long is it reasonable to expect the market to absorb further rate increases? Is there a realistic expectation to boost occupancy in the future? What tactics should be deployed? A significant part of finding the right answers depends on asking the right questions.

Contribution Margin (Net Revenue)

The performance measures discussed so far have worked only with gross room revenue data. None of them has considered expenses. Revenue measures are a good start in revenue management analysis, but they are only a start. The net room revenue calculation is the next level, in which management factors in the most relevant cost item: the variable cost of providing the product (a room night). The variable cost per unit (room night) sold is the added cost incurred to clean, refresh, and resupply a guestroom. This cost is not incurred for unsold rooms. When gross room revenues and variable costs are known, we can calculate the *contribution margin* or *net room revenue*. The contribution margin is the amount of sales revenue left over to contribute to covering fixed costs and, once fixed costs are paid, profit. The formula for a given room's contribution margin is:

$$\text{Contribution margin} = \text{Room rate} - \text{Variable cost}$$

For example, if the room rate is $138 and the variable cost of that room is $18, the contribution margin for that room night is $138 – $18, or $120. Different room types may be priced differently and incur different variable costs. The overall rooms division contribution margin is determined by totaling the margins of the individual rooms.

Identical Net Revenue

One way to apply the contribution margin is by analyzing scenarios with changing price points and occupancy levels. The objective of this calculation is to identify the occupancy percentages that will generate identical net room revenue at changing average rates (ADR). For this example, assume the ADR is $138 and the average variable cost is $18. If current occupancy is 72 percent, what occupancy would be required to generate same net room revenue if we lowered the ADR to $115? The formula is:

$$\text{Required new occupancy} = \frac{\text{Current contribution margin}}{\text{New contribution margin}} \times \text{Current occupancy \%} \times 100$$

$$= \frac{\$138 - \$18}{\$115 - \$18} \times 0.72 \times 100$$

$$= 89.07\%$$

The calculation reveals that this hotel would need 89.07 percent occupancy to generate identical net room revenue if the ADR were lowered from $138 to $115 while the variable cost per room night remained unchanged at $18. The formula works just as well for those scenarios that raise rates. If management in our example were considering an increase to a $143 ADR, an occupancy of 69.12 percent would generate the same contribution margin (net revenue).

This formula helps management to analyze different scenarios by quantifying the possible outcomes of pricing decisions. The revenue manager must determine whether the increase in occupancy that would be needed following a rate reduction would be a realistic goal. In our previous example, a discount of $23 (from $138 down to $115) required a 17 percent boost in occupancy to generate the same net room revenue. Can the hotel make that happen? Management should determine what rate changes would be consistent with the financial obligations of the given hotel in light of supply/demand dynamics. The revenue manager should be best equipped to conduct an analysis of this nature and to help devise a strategy for reaching the budgetary targets of a hotel.

Marginal Revenue Considerations

Marginal revenue is the additional revenue gained from selling one more product unit. *Marginal cost* is the additional cost incurred from selling one more product unit (and is basically another name for a single unit's variable cost). There are two very different situations in which marginal revenue considerations may play a role in room sales. In the first situation, it is assumed and accepted that the hotel is performing well according to its financial objectives (budget) and that it will be able to cover all its expenses as planned. Given these assumptions, a revenue manager interested in maximizing marginal revenues might advocate lowering the prices of unsold rooms to increase unit sales. In this case, the logic is that, as long as the marginal (variable) costs are covered, the rooms department will earn net revenue from such sales. Using the previous example, any room rate over $18 will contribute some net revenue. This is a surprisingly low dollar figure. If a hotel that is on track with regard to its performance targets wishes to generate a buzz in the market with a "super saver special" campaign, this approach is one to consider.

The second situation applies during periods of significant market pressure and might be considered the *contribution margin at any rate* calculation. There are times when extraordinary events result in a large drop in demand. In recent memory, the industry has witnessed such dramatic developments after the September 11, 2001, attacks in New York and Washington, D.C.; after the SARS epidemic in the spring of 2003 in Toronto; and in New Orleans after the tragedy caused by Hurricane Katrina in August 2005, to recall a few. When the market shrinks so quickly, hotels must compete for the business of fewer travelers. In such cases, meeting or exceeding one's budget may become less pressing than simply surviving the downturn. The fixed costs still must be paid, and operations become cash-starved very fast. The thinking is that *any* room rate higher than the variable cost would generate a contribution margin, and any contribution margin is better than none. In order to generate cash flow and maintain the hope of riding out the market slump, a lot of operators resort to this thinking.

GOPPAR

Gross operating profit per available room (GOPPAR) takes the examination of profitability one step further. The GOPPAR calculation compares gross operating profit for a period—a line found on the summary operating statement promulgated by the *Uniform System of Accounts for the Lodging Industry,* Tenth Revised Edition (see Exhibit 2)—to rooms available for that period. The calculation can be done monthly, quarterly, or annually. The formula is:

$$\text{GOPPAR} = \frac{\text{Gross operating profit for a period}}{\text{Available rooms during that period}}$$

For example, a 350-unit hotel with an annual gross operating profit of $4,650,000 would have a GOPPAR of $4,650,000 ÷ (350 rooms × 365 nights), or $36.40.

This measure assesses cost efficiency. While RevPAR is useful to measure revenue performance, there is a growing interest in evaluating overall profitability. Measuring gross profit can expose operational inefficiencies. It is one thing to be able to drive revenue and make the top line of an income statement look impressive. It is another to make the bottom line impressive as well.

The interest in gross operating profit has grown in part because of the proliferation of management contracts over the last couple of decades. The North American hotel industry in particular has embraced the trend of separating hotel ownership from hotel management. That is, it is becoming less common for hotel owners to manage their own hotels. Rather, they hire professional management companies to operate their hotels for a fee. Management contracts have undergone some changes over the years. Most early management contracts based the management company's fee on a percentage of revenue. This approach, however, did not align the interests of the owner and the manager in the most ideal manner. Managers could earn good fees by driving revenue numbers up, even when operational profits were down. One way to address this issue was the introduction of incentive fees based on gross operating profit. Another commonly used term is

Exhibit 2 Summary Operating Statement Format

	Current Period						Year-to-Date					
	Actual		Forecast		Prior Year		Actual		Forecast		Prior Year	
	$	%	$	%	$	%	$	%	$	%	$	%
Revenue[1]												
Rooms												
Food and Beverage												
Other Operated Departments												
Rentals and Other Income												
Total Revenue												
Departmental Expenses[2]												
Rooms												
Food and Beverage												
Other Operated Departments												
Total Departmental Expenses												
Total Departmental Income												
Undistributed Operating Expenses												
Administrative and General												
Sales and Marketing												
Property Operation & Maint.												
Utilities												
Total Undistributed Expenses												
Gross Operating Profit												
Management Fees												
Income Before Fixed Charges												
Fixed Charges												
Rent												
Property and Other Taxes												
Insurance												
Total Fixed Charges												
Net Operating Income												
Less: Replacement Reserves												
Adjusted Net Operating Income												

[1] Departmental Revenue is shown as a percentage of Total Revenue.

[2] Departmental Expenses is the sum of Cost of Sales (when applicable) and Total Expenses. Departmental Expenses are shown as a percentage of their respective department revenue.

Source: *Uniform System of Accounts for the Lodging Industry,* Tenth Revised Edition (Lansing, Mich.: American Hotel & Lodging Educational Institute, 2006), p. 35.

EBIDTA, which refers to earnings before interest, depreciation, tax, and amortization. Look at Exhibit 2 again. Note that every line item above the gross operating profit is the responsibility of the management team, while every line item below gross operating profit is typically the responsibility of the owner. It makes sense to measure management's performance only on those things it can reasonably control. Gross profit calculations and GOPPAR became of interest as a consequence. GOPPAR is also consistent with the objective of revenue maximization strategies and tactics that aim to improve profitability.

Other Measures

There are other measures that can be calculated for the purpose of revenue performance analysis. One is *total revenue per available room (TRevPAR)*. Unlike RevPAR, which uses only room revenue, TRevPAR considers total revenue from all revenue centers. Operators that practice total revenue management will find this a meaningful indicator to track over time.

Another example is *revenue per available customer (RevPAC)*. RevPAC is an indicator that could reveal meaningful information if tracked over time. However, there are significant challenges related to the accuracy of RevPAC. The first challenge is to establish an accurate house count. This is problematic because many hotels do not know precisely how many hotel guests stayed in-house on a given night. There is no universally accepted standard addressing whether double or triple occupancy rooms should command different room rates. Some hotels charge extra per person, others don't. Those that don't will perhaps have less incentive to spend time and effort gathering an accurate count. In some cases, a guest may sign in but may not fill out a registration card if his or her roommate has already signed in.

If the RevPAC calculation is based on total sales revenue, the revenue generated outside the rooms division can become an intriguing issue. Given that this formula is meant to relate revenue to the number of hotel guests, should the revenue include spending by non-guests as well—say, locals patronizing the hotel restaurant? We might believe that this would undermine the accuracy and usefulness of the RevPAC results, but it can be very difficult to accurately separate food and beverage revenues into those generated by guests and those generated by local patrons. Not every check is traceable. Some hotel guests may charge their dinners to their room folios, while others may pay cash. There may be no clear link back to a guest. Similarly, events and catering may produce significant revenue from a local clientele. Should one include that revenue when conducting a RevPAC analysis? These are questions without easy answers. Once the decisions are made, though, perhaps the most important aspect of RevPAC calculations is consistency. After a hotel determines a methodology for its calculations, it should consistently follow that method.

Another calculation that may help a hotel develop an in-depth understanding of its market is the analysis of spending per stay. A hotel has the data to establish how many invoices are paid in a fiscal period from the cashiers' daily reports. The combined total amount of the invoices settled can be divided by the number of payment transactions processed. Actual average dollar spending per customer visits reveals valuable data regarding the clientele of the hotel. The data also expresses the effectiveness of the sales efforts of a given hotel. Mining the data can lead to identifying spending patterns on a variety of revenue streams and other trends.

External Measures

Internal measures compare a hotel's performance with either its own history or its budget. They are critically important, but they do not provide a complete picture on their own. It is also important to look at various external measures. These are measures that compare the hotel with its competitors in the marketplace. A hotel does not exist in a vacuum. Management decisions in one hotel may provoke one or more responses in competing hotels, which in turn may provoke further decisions and adjustments. Most hotels are competing directly for guests with other hotels. To gain a true understanding of a hotel's performance in this dynamic marketplace, one must be able to measure that performance in a meaningful way. This section addresses three important external measures: the competitive set, fair share, and market penetration.

Competitive Set

Once a hotel's management has a clear understanding of its hotel's internal performance measures, it needs to compare its hotel with those hotels it considers to be its competitors. This group of hotels is referred to as the *competitive* or *comp set.* Which hotels belong in the comp set?

Each hotel should identify its competition. Should a budget hotel located on the airport strip consider an upscale downtown hotel a competitor? Probably not. Hotels in close proximity with similar product offerings and rates should generally constitute the comp set. The criteria to define a comp set could be based on a fundamental question: are the hotels included in the comp set targeting the same clientele? Helpful considerations for comp set definition include the following:

- *Geographic location:* A potential guest could see hotels in close proximity as options. In metropolitan markets with a high density, this proximity can be any distance that makes sense, from a couple of blocks to a fifteen-minute driving distance. A hotel revenue manager can locate his or her property on a map and draw a circle around the hotel to identify competitors within a given distance. In rural or resort markets, the distances that need measurement may include not only those to nearby competing properties, but also those for any competing properties that are roughly the same distance from a main point of reference. Hotels located in opposite directions but similar driving distances away from an attraction (say, an airport or a theme park) can easily compete for the same traveler. In resort markets, the distance from the beach or from the ski runs can influence vacationers' hotel selections.
- *Amenities:* Once the geographic boundaries are set, hotels within those boundaries can be added to or eliminated from the comp set based on other criteria. Hotels offering comparable amenities should be considered competitors. Hotels without parking, fitness, and/or convention facilities will have

to decide for themselves whether they compete against properties equipped with those features. Any amenity that is relevant in the eyes of the guest can matter (room service or pay-per-view movie channels, for example). Full-service hotels may target travelers with different needs than limited-service hotels target. Extended-stay hotels may not include a top-tier deluxe-service boutique hotel in their comp set even if located on the same block, as they offer very different amenities and don't vie for the same market segment.

- *Rates:* Price range and price structure both need to be considered. Hotels in the same vicinity with similar amenities and comparable rates mean alternative hotel choices from the guest's point of view. Based on these attributes, it makes sense to include these properties in the comp set. Price structure refers to the existence of similar multi-tiered pricing, perhaps including seasonal rates, government rates, convention rates, and senior rates. Weekend packages and frequent guest discounts can also be part of the comparison. If both the price points and the structure are comparable with a given hotel in the same vicinity, it definitely deserves to be considered a competitor.
- *Ratings.* Rating agencies that award diamonds (AAA/CAA) or stars (Mobile Travel Guide, Canada Select) do a thorough inspection. Potential guests see the same rating in the same locale as a sign of comparable product quality. The rating services carefully look at a variety of attributes, from the curb appeal, maintenance, and cleanliness of the premises to the level of service and competency of the staff. A hotel with the same rating in the same market should be seen as a competitor.
- *Brand affiliation:* Familiarity with a flag can drive decisions, especially in the North American market. This is true even though marketing research shows that there has been substantial erosion in brand loyalty since the late 1990s. Customers appear to be quite willing to abandon a specific brand if a comparable product is available at a more favorable rate. But they usually switch to another brand. In the North American context, most guests prefer a branded product over a non-branded one. Convenience, familiarity, and staying in one's comfort zone are the main reasons for this strong preference. Brand affiliation helps a hotel property connect with its customers. Brands targeting similar segments of the market should be included in the comp set.

Another important consideration in identifying a comp set has to do with Internet search engines and online comparison shopping. Large numbers of potential guests are using these tools to identify their hotel options. It makes sense for a hotel to run similar searches to see what properties come up. Such listings from the most popular search engines and travel websites can confirm existing comp set properties and perhaps reveal competitors that might not yet be part of the comp set. Search engines may use similar criteria to identify potential matches for key words. Better searches offer a selection in listing order by rate, classification, or amenities. Note that most searches are *not organic* (where organic means unbiased, "natural" results solely based on relevant search criteria); service providers can pay to be listed on the first screen or closer to the top of the list, elbowing their way into a more lucrative position on a given list. Nonetheless, such searches are

Industry Insight: Comp Sets

Defining your competition is critical to a hotel's success.
By Scott Farrell, Vice President, TravelCLICK

As you look across your market, define who your competitors are by this measure: "What hotels can I steal share from, and which hotels can steal share from me?" If you aren't sure, ask those making the buying decisions (your guests, travel agents, meeting planners, etc.) what other hotels they are considering for future stays or what hotels they have previously stayed with. Each business segment may have a different set of competitors—for example, transient leisure customers may select from one group of hotels while a meeting planner choosing for a group may choose from among a very different group.

Always measure yourself against your prior performance and against the performance of your competitors. Performance is best measured against the market and competitors. Measuring success solely in relation to a hotel's budget can lead to suboptimal performance. For example, you may be exceeding your budget and thinking things can't get any better, but if the entire hotel market is up, you may not be winning in the market. Remember, a high tide floats all boats. You want to make sure you are rising above your competitors, not with them.

Depending on your market intelligence data, your strategy may be to target sales efforts to specific channels, adjust rates, or fine-tune the timing of your promotions. Establish a plan that helps you achieve your market goals, and put it into action. But don't stop there. Continue to seek market intelligence and adjust your plans based on your findings.

Every hotel competes against someone. Sometimes it is the hotel next door, sometimes it is a hotel across town, and sometimes it is a hotel in another city or state. Too often, the competitive set a hotel uses is poorly defined. Most competitive sets fall into one of two categories:

- Convenient: These are hotels located in a convenient zone, regardless of their actual ability to compete. These competitive sets are generally used to make a hotel look good rather than to gain any market knowledge. With the convenient category, a hotel may appear to be performing well, but not truly understand its place or its opportunity in the market.
- Aspirational: These are hotels the hotel wants to believe it competes against, but doesn't for such reasons as quality, services, or product class. Sometimes, these competitive sets can help a hotel gain market knowledge. More often, though, they cause the hotel to make pricing decisions that ultimately have a negative impact on the hotel.

As you think about your hotel, which competitive set are you using? Look at your current competitive set and ask yourself the following questions:

- Can I reasonably expect to steal business from this hotel?
- Does this hotel consider me a competitor?
- Do my customers consider this hotel when making a buy decision?

(continued)

Industry Insight *(continued)*

Can you answer yes to all three of these questions? If not, it is time to revisit your competitive set and redefine whom you truly compete against. To do this, involve your entire executive team. Visit the hotels in your current comp set and other hotels that offer comparable services or products. Sometimes a hotel needs more than one comp set based on its business mix (such as one for groups and another for transients).

Understanding your comp set will help your hotel define its place in the market and ultimately benchmark itself in a way that shows how it is performing within the market. This is important, regardless of the strength of demand within the market.

In rising markets, a well-defined competitive set will enable your hotel to make sure it is growing at the same pace as or better than the market. And, in declining markets, it will help you make sure your hotel is capitalizing on all of the opportunities available.

Defining which hotels your hotel competes against can help you understand how to sell, market, price, and position your hotel. Once you have properly defined your comp set, what do you do? You should constantly watch what your competitors are doing, how they are selling, and where they are selling. By monitoring activity and positioning yourself competitively, you can capitalize on available opportunities. If you ignore what your comp set is doing, you may either leave money on the table by pricing too low or lose out on market share by pricing too high.

So, how do you leverage your well-defined comp set to make sure you are doing what you should be doing in the market? The easiest answer is to know what is going on. Use competitive data reports to watch your competitors and position your hotel accordingly. On a daily basis:

- Monitor the rates available to consumers for each hotel. This will ensure that you are neither priced too high nor too low for your market. Pricing with the market will enable you to steal share during low-demand periods and drive higher revenues during higher-demand periods. To make this process repetitive, you should invest in a rate-shopping product such as RateVIEW that delivers competitive rate information through a consistent format and process.
- Monitor your pace to make sure rate changes are having the desired effect. If your pace is slowing, you may have been too aggressive with rates. If your pace is increasing too fast, you might want to increase your rates to take advantage of the demand for certain dates.

On a weekly basis:

- Monitor your progress through specific channels. This can be done through your pace report by monitoring pick-up by channel as well as overall pick-up.
- You can also acquire data reports to help monitor your progress through the GDS. The FuturePACE report can help you ensure that the strategies and tactics you are using are having the desired effect.

On a monthly basis, monitor your progress in the marketplace. Many data reports are available. Smith Travel Reports can help you monitor your overall progress against your competitive set. Hotelligence reports can help you understand your position within the GDS against your competitive set. It can also provide valuable sales

Industry Insight *(continued)*

leads that can lead to additional business. Understanding your position can help you determine which of your strategies and tactics are successful and which aren't.

Competitive sets can be valuable resources in understanding your hotel, your marketplace, and your hotel's place in it. By defining a proper comp, watching it, and adjusting it as needed, your hotel can perform better against the comp set regardless of the marketplace—leading ultimately to long-term growth and success. Can you afford not to have a competitive set that works for you rather than against you?

still worthy exercises to do. Revenue managers need to see hotel choices from the traveler's perspective in order to define the comp set accurately.

Markets, and therefore comp sets, are not static by nature. Comp sets need to be reevaluated on a regular basis, at least once a year. After drastic supply and demand changes, a comp set may change quickly. After a sudden drop in demand, for example, it is not unusual to see top-tier properties discount their rates to lure away the guests of mid-tier hotels. Mid-tier properties can suddenly experience competition from hotels that originally were not part of their comp set. A bad storm, a cancelled citywide convention, or the threat of a terrorist attack can turn things on a dime.

As hotel properties change ownership, it is not unusual to see new owners reposition a hotel either up-market (a very ambitious undertaking) or down-market (which is easier and cheaper than a major overhaul). This shift may involve branding a non-branded hotel or re-flagging a branded one. Such changes may redraw the lines in a competitive market and lead to a necessary updating of comp sets.

Comp set definition is vitally important. Every hotel carefully monitors the hotels in its comp set with regard to product improvements, sales campaigns, rate changes, and so forth. Certain actions by competitors will lead a hotel to respond in one way or another. If the comp set has not been carefully determined, it may include hotels that really should not be there. This can become a problem if it leads the hotel to take actions to compete with an ill-identified competitor that really is not targeting the same market. On the other hand, overlooked competing hotels that were wrongly kept out of the comp set may stay under the radar and take significant bites out of a given hotel's market share. Hotels clearly need to define their comp set carefully and maintain the list on a regular basis.

Market Share

Once a hotel has defined its comp set, the next questions to answer are (1) what is the total combined capacity of the competing hotels, and (2) how big is the portion that each competing hotel controls? Some revenue managers describe this as figuring out how big the pie is and how big the slices can get. Consider an example in which five hotels compete for the same market. Assume the following:

Hotel	Number of Rooms	Capacity Market Share
A	205	11.5%
B	225	12.7%
C	400	22.5%
D	460	25.9%
E	485	27.3%
Total	1,775	100%

Each hotel controls an easily calculated portion or share of the combined capacity of 1,775 rooms. The term *fair share* refers to the idea that, all things being equal, each hotel will get a portion of the total market that equals its capacity market share. Every property wants to earn at least its fair share of the market, and preferably more. The following example shows room nights sold during one thirty-day period:

Hotel	Number of Rooms	Capacity Market Share	Room Nights Sold	Room Nights Share
A	205	11.5%	3,936	10.1%
B	225	12.7%	4,590	11.8%
C	400	22.5%	8,520	21.9%
D	460	25.9%	10,626	27.3%
E	485	27.3%	11,204	28.8%
Total	1,775	100%	38,876	100%

The data reveals that hotels A, B, and C hotels did not get their fair share of the room nights. That is, their room nights share is less than their capacity market share. Hotels D and E got more than their fair share: these two hotels were able to get a higher percentage of room nights spent in this market than the capacity share under their control.

But the investigation does not stop with unit sales. Revenue management examines revenue, as well. Consider the following:

Hotel	Number of Rooms	Capacity Market Share	Room Nights Sold	Room Nights Share	Room Revenue	Room Revenue Share
A	205	11.5%	3,936	10.1%	$625,824	12.3%
B	225	12.7%	4,590	11.8%	$679,320	13.4%
C	400	22.5%	8,520	21.9%	$1,158,720	22.8%
D	460	25.9%	10,626	27.3%	$1,285,746	25.3%
E	485	27.3%	11,204	28.8%	$1,333,217	26.2%
Total	1,775	100%	38,876	100%	$5,082,827	100%

Hotels A, B, and C actually exceeded their fair shares of revenue in spite of underachieving in room nights share. On the other hand, hotels D and E were not able to generate room revenue in proportion with their capacity share.

Recall the RevPAR combines occupancy and ADR. It can serve the same purpose in this analysis by combining room nights and room revenue into a single statistic.

Hotel	Number of Rooms	Capacity Market Share	Room Nights Sold	Room Revenue	Occupancy Percentage	ADR	RevPAR
A	205	11.5%	3,936	$625,824	64%	$159	$101.76
B	225	12.7%	4,590	$679,320	68%	$148	$100.64
C	400	22.5%	8,520	$1,158,720	71%	$136	$96.56
D	460	25.9%	10,626	$1,285,746	77%	$121	$93.17
E	485	27.3%	11,204	$1,333,217	77%	$119	$91.63
Total	1,775	100%	38,876	$5,082,827			

A *penetration index* measures chosen indicators in relation to the market averages of the same indicators. An index greater than 100 percent is a measure of a market penetration that exceeds market average. Indexes lower than 100 percent show that the indicator did not reach the market average. A penetration index of 100 percent means that the chosen indicator equals the market average or, in other words, that the hotel achieved an average performance, not better and not worse. To determine market penetration, we need the following calculations:

Market average occupancy percentage = Total room nights sold ÷ Total available room nights × 100
= 38,876 ÷ (1,775 × 30) × 100
= 73.0%

Market average ADR = Total room revenue ÷ Total room nights sold
= $5,082,827 ÷ 38,876
= $130.75

Market average RevPAR = Average market ADR × Average market occupancy percentage
= $130.75 × 0.73
= $95.45

These results allow us to calculate penetration factors for occupancy percentage, ADR, and RevPAR.

Hotel	Capacity: Number of Rooms	Capacity Market Share	Occupancy Percentage	Occupancy Penetration	ADR	ADR Penetration	RevPAR	RevPAR Penetration
A	205	11.5%	64%	79.6%	$159	121.6%	$101.76	106.6%
B	225	12.7%	68%	90.2%	$148	113.2%	$100.64	105.4%
C	400	22.5%	71%	86.2%	$136	104.0%	$96.56	101.2%
D	460	25.9%	77%	106.1%	$121	92.6%	$93.17	97.6%
E	485	27.3%	77%	110.1%	$119	91.0%	$91.63	96.0%
Total	1,775	100%	73%		$130.75		$95.45	

The analysis of RevPAR penetration in this comp set indicates that hotel A is the market leader in terms of RevPAR achievement. How could this hotel establish its leadership position in the comp set? Is it the result of a better website, a more aggressive sales manager, better mattresses, or more attentive guest service? We can only speculate at this point, but revenue managers shouldn't. Product knowledge and market intelligence are important, but before getting into any of those, one should start with the interpretation of hard data and determine what drove RevPAR. The above data set tells the story: the RevPAR penetration of hotel A was driven by the highest ADR penetration, which was able to compensate for the effect of the poorest occupancy penetration in the comp set. The manipulation of the two key variables, rate and occupancy, should be a result of the strategic analysis of the available options. Hotel A chose to drive ADR and got enough market acceptance to achieve 64 percent occupancy, which was enough to make hotel A the RevPAR leader in the comp set.

Considering the performance of hotel E, one can conclude that this hotel chose to drive occupancy instead of ADR. The hotel was fairly successful in this regard, as it was able to grab 28.8 percent of the total room nights during the month. Given the fact that this property controlled 27.3 percent of the room supply in the comp set (the highest), it is fair to observe that hotel E's clout makes it easier to take advantage of this market position as a fairly dominant player within the comp set.

It is always easier to drive rates down to generate cash flow than drive rates up and then back it up with product quality. Although a RevPAR penetration index of 96 percent is nothing to sneeze at, it's a fact that filling a 485-unit hotel (hotel E) is more challenging than filling a 225-unit property (hotel B). Property size and market position are also part of the dynamics resulting in the demonstrated market penetration results per hotel.

At the end of the month, the smallest hotels in the sample comp set achieved the highest RevPAR penetrations, thus realizing their given business potential that month the most effectively. Market performance measured in market penetration is an accurate measure of competitiveness. Revenue managers need to quantify the outcome of strategic decisions through measurements. The examination of the key indicators and understanding what drives them can provide the underpinning of strategy decisions for revenue managers.

The Use of Market Intelligence

A multitude of firms offer services for macro-market information on national and regional data. They also monitor trends and provide forecasts. The best known are STR (Smith Travel Research), PwC (PricewaterhouseCoopers), PKF (Pannell Kerr Forster), and Horwath Consulting. Their big-picture market reports and other publications are useful for hotels that serve a national or international clientele. There are some hotel realty firms that also offer market reports that include useful information that may go beyond the real estate aspects of the industry. HVS (Hotel Valuation Services) and Colliers International are examples of these.

There are also reliable sources that sell specific micro-market information. If accurate data is needed, STR, PKF and TravelCLICK are the highest profile sources in the North American hospitality industry. Their products provide daily, weekly, and monthly data on market performance using key metrics. Subscribers can get reports both on aggregate market data and on a property-specific basis. Self-defined comp set data can also be requested.

The data in the reports can be very informative: the year-to-year, rolling 28 days, rolling 3- and 12-month data sets offer a daily breakdown of property indicators, comp set indicators, and indexes calculated much as demonstrated in this chapter. The ADR data can be provided in major segments like transient, group contract, and others. The revenue can include "other revenue" as well, i.e., revenue beyond room revenue of the hotels in a chosen comp set.

Forecasting and sales information per distribution channel are also available. Each market intelligence provider has a competitive strength, a product or service that may be a worth consideration. Hotel managers should get the most useful information from well-selected sources, as budgetary constraints will always affect purchasing decisions. Purchasing access to relevant market information is vital. A revenue manager can determine the market intelligence needs of a given hotel and identify the best fit to meet them when selecting suppliers. Market intelligence is a critical aspect of well-informed decision making. The money used to acquire the right set of data is well spent.

Market intelligence will provide the data and even some interpretation. But it will still be up to the revenue manager to analyze, interpret, and reflect in order to make wise decisions and choices. The revenue manager needs to involve other managers in this process of gathering data and facts, sifting through and interpreting them, and assimilating them to arrive at wise decisions.[2]

Measurement Challenges

All measurement methods, formulas, calculations, and analyses face some challenges. The most frequently contested issue is the accuracy of claims that attribute a certain improvement in performance to revenue management system implementation. It is reasonable to question whether any improvement in, say, RevPAR penetration or profitability can be conclusively attributed to a systematic practice of revenue management. The points of reference and the yardstick one might want to apply are the first subjects of challenge.

If a given hotel compares its performance measures from before and after the implementation of a systemic approach to revenue management, the following question arises: Can the hotel determine what portion of the changes are the results of applied revenue management and what portion would have happened anyway due to other factors? For example, if a hotel measured a 5 percent increase in year-to-year occupancy, can anyone determine if this was due to revenue management efforts, better training, renovation/refurbishment, new amenities, a redesigned website, new promotions, etc.?

If a given hotel compares its performance measures with another hotel, the following question arises: Can the hotel determine whether a hotel with a revenue management system performs better than a hotel without one? For example, both hotel X and hotel Y consider each other part of their respective comp sets. Hotel X has implemented a revenue management system, while hotel Y has not. After comparing performance measures, there are still valid questions: are the differences related to revenue management practices only or could they be related to differences in service quality? To management's abilities? To location? To room size? To the age difference of the properties? To their brand affiliations?

If a given hotel compares its performance measures to market averages, the following questions arise: Can we determine what portion of the changes are the results of the applied revenue management of one hotel and what changes are the results of seasonal or cyclical fluctuations that would have affected the whole market anyway and are beyond the control of management? For example, if a hotel measures a 7 percent decline in RevPAR compared with a previous fiscal period in a market where the average decline in RevPAR in its comp set was 10 percent over the same period, is it a fair conclusion that the hotel with the smallest rate of decline is the market leader or highest achiever? Can that be attributed solely to revenue management strategies and tactics? How can we tell? If we decide or assume no, what portion of the difference between the given hotel's RevPAR and the aggregate market RevPAR is the result of revenue management strategies and tactics and not some other factors?

There is growing recognition of the positive impact of revenue management on profitability. However, when it comes to accurately quantifying the outcome of systematic revenue management solutions, the accuracy of measurement, tracking, and benchmarking can be problematic.

These issues make the claims of certain vendors and suppliers of revenue management systems equally problematic. Such firms sometimes promise a minimum improvement of *x* percent in revenue or claim a typical minimum net revenue increase of *x* percent from year one. Others describe product benefits as significant, measurable, and quantifiable and offer IRR, ROI, and payback analyses. These claims may in fact be true. However, given the measuring issues just discussed, a vendor and potential user should agree at the outset on exactly what measurements will be used in determining whether the vendor's product met its guarantee. Accurate measurement can help avoid misunderstandings and disputes. It will also help substantiate the improved results of systematic revenue management practices.

Endnotes

1. Smith Travel Research offers STR Global at www.STR.com. They have a selection of market-specific reports (STAR is great example), and they also publish www.hotelnewsnow.com, which is a reliable source of general industry news, trends, insights, reports, and blogs. Another excellent source is TravelCLICK at www.travelclick.net, which has a number of products, e.g. Hotelligence and Rateview. Hotel Valuation Services at www.hvs.com offers market reports based on aggregate data plus relevant articles and archives.

2. Robert Cross discusses the evolution of information, which starts with data (independent facts); in the next stage, it becomes information (the interpretation of data); the next level is knowledge (the assimilation of information); and the ultimate level is wisdom (the optimization of knowledge to make the best decision). See Robert G. Cross, *Revenue Management: Hard-Core Tactics for Market Domination* (New York: Broadway Books, 1997).

References

Banker, Rajiv D., Gordon Potter, and Dhinu Srinivasan. 2005. "Association of Nonfinancial Performance Measures with the Financial Performance of a Lodging Chain." *Cornell Hotel and Restaurant Administration Quarterly* 46 (4): 394–412.

Ingold, Anthony, Una McMahon-Beattie, and Ian Yeoman, eds. 2000. *Yield Management: Strategies for the Service Industries.* 2d ed. London: Thomson Learning.

Kasavana, Michael L., and Richard M. Brooks. 2005. *Managing Front Office Operations.* 7th ed. Lansing, Mich.: American Hotel & Lodging Educational Institute.

Chapter 3 Outline

Competencies

1. Explain how revenue management relies on forecasting and detail elements and components of forecasting that relate to revenue management. (pp. 35–39)
2. Identify and describe the various components of tactical rate management. (pp. 39–49)
3. Identify three tactics that can be used to maximize revenue by controlling the length of guest stays. (pp. 49–51)
4. Define capacity management and how it is used in revenue management. (pp. 51–55)
5. Describe and perform a displacement analysis. (pp. 55–61)

3

Tactical Revenue Management

REVENUE MANAGEMENT AT THE STRATEGIC LEVEL focuses on long-term goals such as identifying desired target markets and identifying or creating factors that differentiate one hotel from its competitors. In contrast, tactical revenue management focuses on operations. Most hospitality operators have practiced tactical revenue management in one way or another. That is, most managers forecast demand, apply multi-tiered rate structures, and run scenarios to compare bookings. Tactical revenue management is in fact how most revenue managers started their careers in the field. Unfortunately, some managers tend to see tactical revenue management as the whole of revenue management. In fact, strategic revenue management offers better, more sustainable revenue positions. Tactical revenue management efforts should support strategic decisions and goals, not undermine them.

Tactical measures are distinctly different from strategic ones. Tactical measures have a relatively short time horizon, usually from same-day to same-quarter issues. Tactical actions are easily quantifiable and measureable, unlike strategic ones. Tactical measures include forecasting, rate management, stay control, capacity management, and displacement analysis.

Forecasting

Forecasting is one of the cornerstones of revenue management. Short-term forecasting provides vital information for tactical revenue management, while long-term forecasting provides the basis for strategic revenue management. Forecasts help management to anticipate periods of constrained and unconstrained demand and to determine expected unit sales and revenue. This information is the foundation for making sound decisions regarding operations management, resource allocation, staff scheduling, and supply chain management. Forecasts will also drive important tactical decisions regarding pricing, group capacity allocation, ideal space configuration, and much more.

It is important to point out the relationship between budgets and forecasts. The budget of a hotel is the document that contains a detailed breakdown of all revenue and expenses reasonably planned and expected for the budget period. The objective of the budget is to document how a given hotel will realize its financial objectives. A budget, once approved, is not likely to change unless dramatic unforeseen events force a revision. A forecast is a projection based on information available at the time of its preparation. This is the best educated guess to help anticipate the quantity of units sold and the revenue generated from those sales. A forecast is not static. It can and should be updated on an ongoing basis as relevant new data becomes available. If the updated forecast suggests that the attainment of budget numbers is in jeopardy, management needs to intervene and decide what course of action to take.

An annual forecast may be revisited on a quarterly basis. A rolling 90-day forecast needs to be revised once a month. A 28-day forecast should be looked at on a weekly or bi-weekly basis, depending on the needs of a given hotel. These needs are affected by the season of the year, the size of the property, and the lead time and booking patterns of targeted markets. If 10-day, 7-day or 3-day forecasts are considered necessary, they should be updated daily.

A long-term forecast (covering 12 or more months) is not expected to be completely accurate. The shorter the term, the more accurate the forecast should become. A 30-day or a 7-day forecast involves less uncertainty than the annual forecast does. Even short-term forecasts are rarely 100 percent accurate, but they can come close. As one approaches the subject period, more and more solid information becomes available regarding competitors, scheduled attendance at events, the weather, year-to-date performance numbers, the pace of booking, and other factors.

Revenue management efforts focused solely on room revenue will rely on room revenue forecasts. Total revenue management efforts will include forecasts for function space and other revenue centers as well.

Forecasting Demand

A long-term demand forecast serves as a framework and a compass to anticipate which direction to turn to and how far one can expect go. While long-term demand forecasting is less detailed and accurate than short-term forecasting, management needs both. The long-term forecast will be based both on historical data and on current key economic indicators (economic growth rate, employment rate, inflation, and indicators related to disposable income) of the hotel's feeder markets. The long-term forecast uses these indicators to anticipate the future economic climate. Will next year's demand will be stronger, weaker, or the same as the current year? If change is expected, it is important to anticipate which segments will show growth or decline, because this information drives the hotel's response. Different tactics are used for different markets.

Short-term forecasts are much more detailed. They provide enough information to justify taking specific actions as they rely on more current and accurate data: daily currency exchange rates, actual travel restrictions, price changes of complementary products (i.e., airfare, gasoline, tolls, and fees) and substitute products (such as other hotels), visitor statistics, the quantifiable impact of the latest market trends, etc. Short-term demand forecasts will not likely affect strategic directions, but they can confirm chosen strategies and help refine chosen tactics.

A short-term forecast will identify demand generators with names and numbers (what convention has how many registrations, which tour operator booked how many bus tours for a trade exhibition, which new show opened successfully and how many performances are scheduled next month, which local sports franchise has made the next round in a playoff run, etc.). The margin of error is smaller, the cutoff dates are known, and historical data can help in forecasting wash and spill factors if an event has past history on file. (In a group context, *wash factor* refers to group members who check out early rather than stay the entire length of the event. *Spill factor* refers to the number of rooms set aside in the group block that do not sell to members of the group by the agreed-upon cut-off date; these rooms can then be released from the group hold and sold to others.)

Short-term forecasts are also more *granular*. Granularity means breaking forecast information down into clusters—for example, by market segment, price category, and/or duration of stay. Forecasts can be broken down by reservation channels (voice, Internet, or global distribution systems) and by reservation methods (direct to guest, chain's call center, or third-party) as well.

The analysis of reservation inquiries helps revenue managers understand trends in call volume changes, conversion rates, and reasons for regrets and denials. (In reservation terminology, a *regret* is a potential guest who decides not to book; a *denial* is a potential guest turned away because of a lack of available space.) For example, reservation agents can log all inquiries, not just those calls that were converted into sales. The analysis of regrets and denials can provide useful information regarding price resistance or customer needs and wants. The captured portion of demand is easier to track accurately than the uncaptured portion.

Constrained and Unconstrained Demand. Demand is considered *unconstrained* when a hotel can fully meet the total demand. This typically happens in low seasons. Hotels are unlikely to place restrictions on guests wishing to reserve rooms during periods of unconstrained demand. However, once demand levels rise above the hotel's capacity to meet it fully, demand becomes *constrained*. Only a certain portion of demand can be accommodated. In this situation, the hotel may place various conditions or constraints on the sale of rooms to which prospective guests must agree in order to book the rooms. The most frequently applied constraints are capacity allocation, rate thresholds, and stay (duration) control.

From a revenue management perspective, if total demand exceeds a hotel's ability to meet it, the hotel should be selective and capture the highest-yield portion of it. Interestingly, this does not always mean booking the guests willing to pay the highest room rates. Room rates are only one element of the total yield a customer provides. The concept of *total spend* considers all revenue (rooms, food and beverage, function space, etc.) and is not restricted to considering a single visit in isolation. A broader-based strategic approach considers the *lifetime total value* of a guest or a client organization instead of the price point of a given room on a given day. For example, if a hotel could sell a room on a given day for (say) $50 more to guest A than guest B, does that justify denying the reservation to guest B? What if guest B is a frequent, loyal guest who spends on more than rooms? A guest who visits a hotel three times a year, stays multiple days, and spends on food and beverage, parking, function space rental, and entertainment is likely to be more valuable (provide a higher total yield) than an unknown guest (one with no history of staying at the hotel) with a one-night reservation who agrees to pay $50 more for that one night. It would be a mistake to displace a higher total yield guest in favor of a lower yield guest. In practice, this means that revenue managers should *not* simply treat each day as a separate and distinct opportunity to maximize the daily revenue total. Revenue maximization is a long-term process, and decisions made on one day can have effects on many other days. It may seem counterintuitive, but there will likely be times when it makes better revenue management sense to turn down higher paying guests or clients for a given night or event if accepting that business jeopardizes likely future business.

In other words, room rates are important, but they are not absolute measures. Revenue management has to maximize profitability by factoring in all available relevant revenue data. Revenue managers can improve the profitability of the whole hotel, not just the revenue of the rooms division.

Pace of Build. The *pace of build* is another important indicator in demand forecasting. Revenue managers can compare the booking pace of the current year with those of previous years. It is important to start with historical data. However, it is also important to consider current conditions and to factor in changes in booking patterns. A significant change taking place now is the shortening of lead times for all segments.

Consider the following booking pace example showing actual group room bookings for July 20X1 and actual group room bookings through April for July 20X2 sales.

	Total Group Room Bookings, Cumulative by Month						
	January	February	March	April	May	June	July
20X1	350	680	740	860	880	920	890
20X2	360	690	700	750			

The booking pace shows that 20X2 had started stronger than the previous year. Based on the January and February data, the hotel was on pace to meet or exceed 20X1's volume for July. During March and April, the pace of build slowed and the hotel has 110 fewer nights booked in April for the month of July than at the same time the previous year. A revenue manager would need to respond to this situation by either going more aggressively after the group market or reallocating some rooms being held open for group business to one or more other market segments.

In order to interpret the data correctly, the revenue manager must know that lead times differ for different segments of the market. Events (festivals, sport tournaments, conventions, etc.) need significantly more planning and preparation time than vacation trips. Groups have longer lead times than individual trips. Long-haul travel markets have longer lead times than near-market travel markets. Reservation managers have to know intimately well the booking patterns of their feeder markets.

For some markets, the shortening of lead times and the growing number of last-minute bookings have a lot to do with changing lifestyles and travel habits.[1] In the United States, the average length of vacations is getting shorter, and these shorter vacations are taken more frequently than before. The ease of access to travel information coupled with the ability to make instant online transactions feeds this consumer trend. Consumers also have noticed the prevalent revenue management practice of discounting distressed inventory. More and more travelers take advantage of special deals offered by airlines, cruise lines, car rental companies, resorts, and hotels that attempt to offload unsold inventory by capturing demand from flexible last-minute bookers.

Carefully monitoring the pace of build will help revenue managers to avoid the "fire sale" of unsold inventory at heavy discounts. Group booking pace can be a useful early indicator of the future market demand trends due to its longer lead time. Timely intervention can be started relatively early if the booking pace gives reason for concern.

Forecasting Room Availability

The forecasting of room availability for any future date starts with the number of available units. That number is then adjusted to account for the various factors that will affect the number of rooms available for sale on the date in question. From total rooms, we subtract rooms already occupied by previous arrivals staying beyond the day in question (stayovers), any rooms that are out of order, expected arrivals of the given day, expected walk-ins, and guests who are scheduled to check out but extend their stay (overstays). A hotel cannot know with certainty how many walk-in guests will show up on a given day, nor can it know in advance which or how many guests are likely to extend their stays. But the hotel can look at its historical records and make educated estimates for planning purposes. After subtracting all these elements, the forecaster adds in expected cancellations, expected no-shows, and expected early departures (understays). Again, these numbers cannot be known in advance with certainty, but percentages can be reasonably estimated from historical data.

The calendar date is a good starting point when mining historical data, but the day of the week is just as important. For example, the current year's July 8 forecast may consider the previous year's July 8 figures, but if last year July 8 fell on a Thursday and this year it is a Friday, the comparison may not be as useful, especially to a hotel with very different weekday and weekend occupancy patterns. In this case, it will likely be more appropriate to look at the second Thursday in July for comparison.

How far into the future does a revenue manager forecast room occupancy? The most frequently prepared forecasts are 3-day, 5-day, weekly, 10-day, monthly, quarterly, and annual forecasts. Each revenue manager will choose a system best suited to a given property based on markets and property types.

Tactical Rate Management

Many people consider rate management to be the heart and soul of revenue management. Managers who hold a simplistic view of revenue management often wrongly perceive price control as revenue management itself. Revenue management involves much more than rate control. Nonetheless, the pricing of the room night is a pivotal issue that has both tactical and strategic aspects.

The strategic approach to pricing has a longer term view. Its main objective is revenue growth through successful price positioning in a given comp set and through maintaining or growing market share. On balance, the tactical approach to room rate management has a short-term operational focus that considers same-day and same-week rate management issues. Its main objective is cash flow generation from revenue growth.

A hotel's tactical rate management should align with its strategic pricing approach. Inconsistencies between tactical and strategic pricing spell trouble. If, for example, a hotel positions itself as a pricey upper-upscale property with high service quality (a strategic choice) and then reacts to a market hiccup by offering huge discounts and other significant incentives (two-for-ones, double loyalty points, and the like), these tactical measures would seriously undermine the integrity of the hotel's strategic positioning. A deviation like this from strategic objectives also makes it very hard to maintain the coveted upper-tier image and rates.

The strategic rate level and market position that are the results of dedicated efforts and hard work can be very easily compromised by wrong tactical choices. It is not that unusual to see four-diamond full-service hotels suddenly going head-to-head against three-diamond limited-service hotels. If they become cash starved during a market slump, higher-ranked hotels may choose to compete on price by offering a better value at comparable price points. This desperate measure will probably cost them more than the revenue gain grabbed from other properties. Diluting a brand name and devaluing a product have consequences. Revenue managers should think carefully before they decide to go after a market segment that has never been theirs and that, if the market recovers, will never be considered as a target again. Discounting has not proven to be a successful method of RevPAR growth. The consistency of tactics and strategy is a lot more important than most managers would like to admit.

What revenue managers need to consider is that customers prefer clarity: they prefer to know what they can expect from a given brand or service provider. At the least, this means rate level, amenities, and service quality. Consistency in these categories means a lot to guests. Hotels that never deviate from their positioning, never jerk their rates too far up and down, and keep the same target markets every season are rewarded with a steadier flow of revenue and a more loyal customer base.

Tactical rate management requires a multi-tiered rate structure. What is a rate structure and what is not? If different room types are priced differently in a hotel, that reflects a certain selection rather than a rate structure. Differences in room size, location, view, and so forth may and should be reflected in rates (physical rate fences). In contrast, a multi-tiered rate structure means that the same room night can be sold at varying price points.

Some hotels can afford to have a very simple pricing approach. For example, a solitary roadside motel located at the off-ramp of a major highway may deal exclusively with traveling guests who arrive without reservations and never stay more than one night. This motel might have one rate only and would sell the first room of the night at the same rate as the last room that completes a full house. This operator may never need or want to practice revenue management. On the other hand, most hotels in competitive, saturated markets choose a more complex approach to pricing their room nights to reflect seasonality and the fact that their clienteles are not necessarily homogeneous.

Rate Structure

A rate structure can be as complex or as simple as the hotel believes makes the most sense. Hotel A may offer nine different rates for the same room, while hotel

B offers 16 and hotel C offers 39. A surprising number of revenue managers may have two dozen or more. There is no conclusive evidence that 39 different rates work better than 16. One might wonder if there are really 39 distinctly different clusters of guests that a given hotel might want to cater to.

Is there a meaningful difference between a room rate of, for example, $158 and $155? How can one characterize the buying behavior differences associated with a $3 rate difference in the $150–$160 range? If this difference would really make or break a possible sale, then by all means a revenue manager should consider it. However, a manageable system with well defined and distinctly different offerings would make much more sense. The differences between price points should be a reflection of buying behavior, customer needs, and purchase power balanced with the perception of value from the guests' perspective.

Rack Rate. The *rack rate* is the highest rate a hotel would like to charge for unconstrained demand. It is also referred to as the walk-in rate, the premium rate, and the posted rate. This is the rate that is quoted first when a potential guests asks, "Do you have a room for tonight?" Most jurisdictions require hotels to display each room's rack rate conspicuously inside the room. According to research, more than 80 percent of guests claim they try to negotiate a lower room rate than the one quoted.[2] The research also noted that potential guests often try to get all the perks and extras without paying extra. A rack rate is the rate that most guests would like to bargain down. The chances of collecting the rack rate will depend on supply and demand. A hotel is in a stronger bargaining position to hold its rack rate in periods of excess demand.

A statistic known as the *rate achievement factor (RAF)* measures the hotel's efficiency in achieving the rack rate. The calculation of rate efficiency can be done by comparing actual ADR for a room type to the rack rate for that room type. For example, if a room type has a rack rate of $120 and an ADR of $84, the RAF is $84 ÷ $120, or 70 percent. The RAF indicates how heavily the rack rate was discounted in a given period and serves as a constant reminder that we are now living in an age of comparison shopping, price transparency, and well-informed, hard-bargaining customers.

The term rack rate originated from the days when there was a physical room rack at the front desk of hotels. Today, hotels with actual room racks are hard to find. Computerized property management systems (PMS) are affordable and user friendly enough that even small operators can buy and use them. The PMS assigns rate codes to all the different rates a hotel would have, with rack rate as the top rate. All other rates are lower, and that means some form of a discount for one reason or another.

Corporate and Special Corporate Rates. Transient hotels offer volume discounts to provide an incentive for potential buyers of a lot of room nights. While leisure travelers spend after-tax or discretionary income to travel and are more price sensitive than business travelers, leisure travelers usually lack the purchase power to justify a special rate. Corporate travelers are a lot less price sensitive for a variety of reasons, but corporations have more leverage as volume purchasers. Corporations having a lot of business activity in a given locale are in a good position to negotiate preferential treatment.

Corporate rate as a category can include many corporate rates based on the volume of room nights. If a corporation will buy enough room nights per year to qualify for a corporate discount, the hotel will generally offer a basic corporate rate. If the volume is significant enough to warrant an even greater discount, a preferred corporate rate is customary. Corporations that have a manufacturing plant, a headquarters, a training facility, or a main unit in the hotel's vicinity can provide a significant and more or less steady need for hotel rooms over the years. In such cases, a corporate-specific rate can be negotiated—for example, an IBM rate, a Ford rate.

There are also special corporate deals in the form of contract rooms. A good illustration is an airline that needs 12 rooms every night. The airline personnel alternate and will check in and check out as they need to. The hotel will invoice the airline as agreed. The assigned rooms will always be available, and a contract will govern the fixed amount charged for the rooms and the frequency of invoicing.

The negotiation of a corporate rate can happen at a property level or at a corporate (chain) level. A certain annual volume of room nights can be included in an agreement. From management's perspective, it is important to work out the fine details: who qualifies for the corporate rate (employees only or business associates as well)? Is there a dedicated position or office to coordinate and place bookings? What room type is offered? Are there seasonal rate adjustments? Is the same rate recognized on holidays or high-demand citywide event days? Are there blackout dates? Is there a required minimum lead time per booking?

Another important issue that can arise has to do with who has priority. Suppose a reservations manager determines that she could get the rack rate for all the rooms normally allotted to corporate guests for the coming week. She wants to do it because higher rates mean more revenue. The real question for a revenue manager is, what is more profitable for the hotel? Guests who enjoy a corporate rate have history that can be analyzed. Such guests may come at a lower room rate, but spend more in the hotel's other revenue centers than typical transient guests. Even if they don't, though, there may be more at stake. A revenue manager can determine a corporate account's total annual room nights and revenue generated and compare this with the minor revenue increase that could be achieved by turning away corporate guests in favor of rack-rate-paying guests during the coming week. Based on the larger picture, the answer is usually quite clear. Turning away corporate guests could endanger the corporate account. It does not make good business sense to lose a significant volume of revenue in the long term just to get a small increase in revenue in the short term. Short-term objectives and long-term objectives need to be aligned. Short-term thinking can be dangerous in a business like a hotel that is built for the long haul.

Note that hotels sometimes offer last-minute discounts to the public that are lower than their corporate rates. Corporate travelers who notice this may object and point out they could have paid a lower rate if they had held out until last minute. They might feel abused rather than rewarded for the loyalty shown to the hotel. They might even question the need for a negotiated corporate discount when travelers can get lower rates without any demonstrated loyalty. Hotels, on the other hand, feel they deserve some flexibility in order to have blackout dates or the opportunity not to honor negotiated corporate rates on occasion.

They question the rationale of charging a corporate room rate much lower than the going ADR on excess demand days when comparable hotels may be sold out charging premium rates. These considerations have led more and more hotels and corporate partners to negotiate a certain percentage off the best available rate (BAR) as a corporate discount instead of a fixed corporate rate. Those operators who practice dynamic rate management (discussed later in this chapter) benefit most from this approach by gaining additional flexibility in tactical rate control without irritating loyal corporate clients.

Group Rates. The significance attributed to group revenue in a given hotel is a strategic decision. Whatever the strategic approach to group business might be, the tactical measures require a selective pricing approach consistent with the specific nature of this segment. Group bookings are usually handled by the sales department, where agents and managers are highly specialized in dealing with this line of customers. The revenue manager and the director of sales and marketing need daily coordination and a close working relationship to succeed in revenue maximization.

Selling many room nights at once instead of selling the same number one booking at a time is a lot less resource intensive and costly. It also generates more revenue per booking on the sales side.

Group rates depend on a number of variables, including the season of the year, the number of room nights wanted (based on group size and duration), other revenue (food and beverage, function room rentals, AV, golf, spa, etc.), and the group's history.

The group business segment has a number of sub-segments: corporate meetings, conventions, associations, incentive groups, leisure groups, and SMERF groups (social, military, educational, religious and fraternal organizations). There are also ad-hoc groups (such as a circle of friends for a bachelor party or an alumni reunion that does not happen each year and has no plans returning to the same hotel again) and series groups (such as a bus tour operator arriving each Tuesday for two nights between April and October with overseas tourists).

Group contracts govern room rates, as well as catering and other items. Revenue managers need to consider the margins on each revenue stream. Some group clients bargain hard for a lower room rate, but are more flexible in accepting additional charges (like baggage handling), while others may accept a somewhat higher room rate, but negotiate for inclusive services like breakfast, drink coupons, transportation, and so on.

Promotional Rates. Certain organizations can significantly influence buying. Automobile associations (such as AAA/CAA), organizations representing retired persons (such as AARP), and the publishers of coupon books (such as Entertainment Coupon Book) will negotiate a discount on behalf of their membership, typically in the form of a percentage off the rack rate. Hotels are usually allowed to exclude the highest occupancy dates of the year, when the hotel has the right to charge full rates to qualifying members.

Government Rate. Municipal, provincial/state, and federal governments employ tens of thousands. Their need for accommodation while traveling on business provides a significant revenue source for some hotels. Hotels that are interested in catering to this market will have to honor the government-set rate established for each fiscal year. Negotiations are not necessary, because the government will issue its own directives of per diem spending limits for each budget cycle per market. Note that rates and per diems can vary by location in response to differences in the cost of living.

Event Rates. In North America, it is fairly common that meeting planners are in charge of event management. Professional meeting planners are experienced and knowledgeable regarding the accommodation industry and the complexity of a contract. Event rates may fluctuate based on seasonality and the size and overall revenue impact of the event in question.

A meeting planner may negotiate a room rate as a key element of a contract for a given event that is strongly related to other revenue streams (function room rental, catering, beverage purchase, etc.). Revenue managers need to consider the total revenue impact of an event with a clear understanding of the profitability of the different revenue streams. Based on how it is spent, the same total revenue amount can have very different margins.

Employee Rate. Most hotels charge a discounted rate to employees on business and/or employees on a vacation trip if staying at a hotel of the same brand or corporation. The rates and corporate policies vary and employee or "Friends and Relatives Rates" are always subject of availability.

Complimentary Rate. Offering free accommodations to clients, potential clients, and dissatisfied guests is considered a cost of doing business. A room night can be made complimentary on the spot to help mollify an unhappy guest. Sometimes the offer of a complimentary future stay is more practical.

Promotional campaigns sometimes offer accommodations in exchange for publicity. Some brands use complimentary room nights as a reward to their employees. Some hotels offer room nights as a product donation to support causes and charitable events.

Hotels may also use comp rooms if employees need overnight accommodation when given a back-to-back shifts or when weather emergencies prevent employees from getting home safely.

Hurdle Rate and Best Available Rate. Traditionally, the *hurdle rate* has been the lowest rate a hotel is willing to offer on a given day or week. It may be a flexible amount, as rates may fluctuate under varying market conditions. There may be different hurdle rates on Monday and Friday of the same week, subject to market changes and the cash flow needs of a given fiscal period.

As industry jargon, the term hurdle rate is currently in the process of being replaced by the *best available rate (BAR)*, a newer term that means nearly the same thing. In fact, the terms are often used interchangeably today, even though they have slightly different connotations. (Strictly speaking, the hurdle rate was more static because hotels held information, pricing, and positional power over customers. They could determine a lowest price point and were able to hold firm. As customers have come in recent years to hold much more information power than in the past, the industry's approach to pricing has shifted. The BAR gradually took over as a rate that a service provider believes is the lowest price point that offers an attractive enough value proposition to generate a sufficient volume of business. Unlike the hurdle rate, however, a BAR can be quickly and easily adjusted if dynamic market conditions justify the change. In practical application, the BAR is the best price until something forces a hotel to rethink it.)

A hotel may also use a *stay-sensitive hurdle rate.* This tactic's objective is to maximize revenue generation by offering price incentives for longer stays. The simple principle is that the longer a guest agrees to stay, the lower the nightly hurdle rate will get. The BAR for a one-night stay might be quoted as $140, but if the guest agrees to stay two nights, a BAR of $129 will be offered. A three-day stay might get a BAR of $115. These price options should be pointed out at the time of booking. Guests who accept the option generate higher total revenue at lower unit prices. Unfortunately, most guests show little flexibility with their dates. Travel arrangements are often already finalized by the time a guest begins booking the accommodations portion of a trip. The guest's lack of flexibility in travel arrangements will often limit the effectiveness of this tactical measure.

Tactical Discounting

Discounting in the tactical context is done to generate revenue in the short term. If a hotel believes that downward rate adjustments will provide price incentives for their potential guests to book same-day or same-week room nights, this tactic may help to hold or boost occupancy. However, it must be recognized that selling more room nights at reduced room rates will not necessarily generate higher room revenue. The unknown variable is how much occupancy will be gained at the reduced rate.

Enz, Canina, and Lommano analyzed data of more than 6,000 hotels regarding the effects of discounting from 2001 to 2003.[3] According to their key findings, hotels can increase market share within their comp set by discounting, but it is done at the cost of declining revenue performance. Hotels that chose to discount their rates by more than 2 percent compared with their comp set's average achieved lower RevPAR performance than their competitors. There were minor differences identified in the level of price sensitivity (elasticity) between the clienteles of upper-upscale and economy hotels. In 2003, Canina and Carvel concluded from data of 480 hotels in 22 U.S. metropolitan areas covering 1989–2000 that, on average, for every 10 percent decrease in room rates, demand rose by only 1.3 percent.[4] The evidence to date clearly shows that discounting room rates does not improve profitability.

These findings were also was consistent with research pointing out that the corporate segment is less likely than the leisure segment to respond to a room rate discount.[5]

Overall, it appears that tactical discounting can accomplish a number of things. It can fill rooms that would have stayed vacant. It can steal market share from competitors. It can attract mostly leisure travelers, who are more likely to respond to discounts and perceptions of a better deal. It can get the business of brand neutral, price-sensitive customers. But it does all this by reducing revenue and diluting RevPAR, as the impact of selling more units at lower rates is usually negative.

Late discounting has led to another noticeable and unfortunate trend. More and more guests with reservations are calling to cancel their rooms one or two days before arrival if last-minute discounts have been offered either on third-party websites or on the hotel's website for the date they were booked. They cancel the old reservation, then make a new one at the newly available discounted rate. What has become evident is that a significant portion of guests never stops looking for deals, even after they have booked their room nights. Hotels that post discounts for last-minute bookings may watch already booked business become less profitable when attentive guests discover and switch to the lower rate. This revenue "leakage" may further dilute room revenue.

Despite its often negative impact, the discounting tactic is still frequently used to sell distressed inventory. When a weekly, 3-day or same-day forecast shows fairly disappointing demand, the revenue manager may believe the only way to boost occupancy is to drop rates as a last effort. Demand-based dynamic pricing (discussed in the next section) is applied in order to gauge what price point the market would accept.

Given the drawbacks of discounting, we might reasonably wonder why any revenue manager would ever use it as a tactic. The answer can be complex. Low occupancy has always been considered a reflection of less than satisfactory sales performance. Low occupancy reduces a hotel's ability to pay its fixed costs as they come due, so owners tend to want some sort of intervention to ensure those costs will be covered. The factor that managers can most easily control is room rates, so it is often their first choice—even though discounting should probably be their last choice. Developing a convincing value proposition by creating more value without discounting is harder work: package development (bundling), better defined differentiation, better websites, product improvements like better service, better mattresses, better shower heads, better amenities, better breakfasts, etc. all require more work, more creativity, and need some ramp-up time to take effect. Owners may put pressure on revenue managers to show short-term results, and holding or boosting occupancy through discounting may temporarily assuage owners and get them off the manager's back.

Another argument is that, although room revenue is likely to fall, the increased occupancy may generate larger revenue increases in the hotel's other revenue centers. Increasing occupancy also helps maintain the level of employment the hotel needs to uphold service quality and sustain staff morale. Stealing market share can also be a consideration, but this goal presents a serious issue to deal with. Can a hotel retain the stolen clientele? The answer is probably not. The deal-driven bargain hunters always go where the best deals are. There is no protection against a competitor's steeper discount next time. So even if one day a battle can be won, there is no chance to win a war by using this weaponry. Any price can be undercut by someone more desperate.

There are times when discounting is used for entirely the wrong reasons. After the dramatic events of September 11, the New York hotel market saw a drastic decline in demand. Following the SARS outbreak in the spring of 2003, the bottom of the market fell out in Toronto. In both cases, the steep decline in demand had nothing to do with the pricing level of hotel rooms. Travelers stayed away for a variety of reasons, but high room rates were not one of them. Why would hoteliers expect heavy discounting to fix a problem when room rates were not part of the problem in the first place? If travelers avoid an area because of safety, security, or health concerns, can low rates really persuade them to disregard those concerns? The answer seems obvious. Nonetheless, discounting became so rampant in both cities that it took years for their hotel markets to recover.

By definition, at the day-to-day operational level, hotels take a tactical approach to rate management versus a strategic one.[6] But tactics should not ever ignore the larger strategy. To avoid confusing the market by saying one thing and doing another, strategy and tactics should be aligned. Unfortunately, many managers use tactics that conflict with the larger strategy. When we see hotel brands that promote service quality as their strategic choice for market positioning start to discount and promote value instead in their day-to-day operations, there is a clear misalignment. Driving attention to discounts will undermine a coveted strategic choice of being a service quality differentiated brand—a market position that takes extended effort to achieve. Consumers should not be confused: brand clarity is vital. If a hotel chooses to be a price or value driven choice, it should support that strategy consistently with its tactics.

All of this does *not* mean that discounting should never be used. However, managers who consider tactical discounting need to understand the complexity and dangers of the issue.

Dynamic Pricing

Dynamic pricing means that a hotel will change its room rates daily or even within a day if up-to-the-minute market information reveals the need for adjustments. It is based on the recognition that the right rate to charge for a room night is what the customer is able and willing to pay. By underpricing, the revenue manager leaves money on the table; by overpricing, the hotel may price itself out of the market. Those who practice dynamic pricing believe that the hotel has to continually adjust rates in response to ever changing supply/demand conditions. The constant challenge, of course, is trying to determine the optimal price on a given day or afternoon.

A very popular pricing principle that applies dynamic pricing is called *demand-based pricing*. In low-demand periods, lower rates are offered. As demand increases, lower rate categories are closed and higher rates are quoted. Demand-based pricing as a principle is not new. Its prevalent use today has been made possible by high-speed connectivity, broadband integrated networks, and lightning-speed data processing. Revenue managers can keep their fingers on the pulse of the market, since a lot of information can now be accessed in real time. Room rate adjustments can be implemented at the click of the mouse, and updated rates can be posted across multiple distribution channels with ease.

A simple example will help to demonstrate the difference between dynamic, demand-based pricing and static pricing. Assume, for example, that on a given day, the 300-room Astoria Hotel sells 250 rooms. In scenario A, the hotel has two-tiered pricing with a group rate of $90 and a transient rate of $130. In scenario B, the hotel has multi-tiered pricing: a low-demand rate of $90 and other rates of $110, $130, and $150, offered at increasing occupancy levels. Both scenarios sell the same number of total rooms, with sales at each rate broken down as follows:

A: Rate	Group Rate $90	Transient Rate $130	Total
Rooms sold	150	100	250
Revenue	$13,500	$13,000	$26,500

B: Rate	$90	$110	$130	$150	Total
Rooms sold	80	60	60	50	250
Revenue	$7,200	$6,600	$7,800	$7,500	$29,100

In comparing scenarios A and B, note that B produced $2,600 more in revenue, an ADR increase of $10.40, and a RevPAR increase of $8.67. In scenario B, the revenue manager closed the $90 rate after 80 rooms were booked and set the rate $110. After 60 more rooms were booked, this rate was closed and the next 60 rooms were booked for $130. When the next 60 units were booked and hotel had 200 rooms booked, a rate of $150 was offered for the last 50 bookings. This approach increased room revenue, ADR, and RevPAR by 9.8 percent without selling more units.

Dynamic pricing does not adjust room rates only upward or only downward. Price changes can go either way. Assume a revenue manager has forecasted 75 percent occupancy for the day, but she opens the day looking at only 65 percent ROB (rooms on the book) with a $160 BAR. She wonders if that missing 10 percent occupancy can be realized from walk-ins and same-day bookers. By early afternoon, there is no demonstrated new demand out there at the posted rate. At 2 P.M. she decides to intervene. She lowers the BAR to $139. The phone lines start buzzing. By 6 P.M., the hotel has picked up enough same-day bookings to expect 80 percent occupancy. By shopping her comp set, she learns that some of the other hotels are starting to sell out of certain room types. The revenue manager at this point decides to change tactics. At 6:15 P.M., she closes down the discounted rate and posts a new rate for walk-ins of $170. Such is dynamic pricing at work.

How dynamic must one become to be dynamic *enough*? There are no simple answers. The above example raises many questions. Would the originally forecasted occupancy have been achieved without dynamic pricing, just by staying the course with the starting BAR of $160? Did the hotel encounter price resistance or resentment from guests who had booked their room at the higher rates?

There are arguments for and against frequent price changes. A revenue manager will weigh the notion of consistency and price integrity against possible revenue gains through frequent tweaking. There is also the issue of "who's in charge?" Should revenue managers stress consistency or should they go with the flow and let the perceived market forces dictate pricing levels? Are a hotel's service quality, location, brand name, and amenities worth suddenly much less or much more just because market demand shifted one afternoon?

There are dangers in approaching rate controls with a narrow perspective that focuses on one key variable only—usually occupancy. If a hotel reacts to surpassing 80 percent occupancy by closing out its government rate while not forecasting to fill, that decision can be questionable. If, for example, a government-related event takes place in the region and the hotel stops honoring that rate, revenue

Industry Insight: Dynamic Pricing

By Bill Winzer, Vice President, Pricing and Analysis, Marriott International

Dynamic pricing can be a very effective approach to maximizing hotel performance. The key to dynamic pricing is to understand the projected demand for your hotel, overall demand for the market, and demand in your local competitive set.

As demand-changing events occur (group bookings, severe weather, etc.) at your hotel and the competition, the revenue leader needs to determine the impact of the event and any pricing or rate program restrictions that need to be modified.

You must be careful also to understand the pricing and mix of business of your competition. If a competitor raises its benchmark rate, you need to know how much of its business is being sold at these price points. Just because a competitor raises its price point does not mean it is correct. You need to be aware of any pricing changes by your key competitors, fully understand the positioning of your hotel, and make the appropriate pricing changes.

For example, a 200-room hotel was forecasting 90 percent occupancy for a three-day time period. The hotel sales team just booked a corporate group with a strong catering contribution that exceeded the group target rates and contribution over this time period. The hotel has just gone from an unconstrained forecast of 90 percent to 120 percent. Based on this booking, the revenue leader would review the forecasted transient demand by segment and determine what length of stay of restrictions should be applied during this week and if any increase to the benchmark rate is appropriate. All premium rooms would be strongly promoted during these high-demand days. The goal of the pricing and length-of-stay restrictions is to increase revenue and profit for the entire week, not just on the three forecasted sellout nights.

opportunities will not be maximized. If demand came mostly from that particular segment, competitors that keep their government rate open may pick up the rejected volume. The point is to be selective in closing rate categories. Look beyond the volume of demand to see segment dynamics as well before applying rate controls.

Should a given hotel compete on price? That is a strategic decision. If a revenue manager makes a considered decision to use pricing as a competitive weapon, dynamic rate management can become one of the most effective tools in the battle for price-sensitive customers.

Stay (Duration) Control

One revenue maximization tactic is to select the highest yield reservations from among all inquiries by managing the availability of the product. The assumption is that longer stays equal higher yields. The application of *stay control* (also called *duration control*) means that instead of offering rooms on a "first-come-first-served" basis, the hotel attaches conditions to its room offers. Reservations that don't meet those conditions are rejected, even if rooms are still available.

Minimum-Stay Requirements

Minimum-stay requirements are one such condition. During periods of excess demand, revenue managers can restrict room sales to those guests who agree to stay a minimum number of days. If a multi-day event attracts guests expected to stay many nights, accepting shorter reservations may prevent a hotel from selling from those rooms to longer-staying guests who call later. For example, the New York City Marathon is traditionally run on a fall weekend and it attracts many thousands. Most local hotels require a minimum of two nights based on the event's historic impact on the city's accommodation industry. Similarly, resorts that sell one-week packages may not be interested in accepting shorter bookings in peak season. The objective of this tactic is to maximize revenue by accepting bookings that produce higher yields based on stay pattern forecasting.

A possible downside of this tactic is that high lifetime value guests may be rejected. It should be possible for hotel staff to use discretion with such guests and override a given system's stay controls. It may be a very good idea to log and track rejected bookings to make sure the tactic is not misapplied or used counterproductively. Corrective measures can be taken if data shows minimum-stay requirements are leading to undesirable levels of lost revenue.

Stay Through

On occasion, there are gaps in the forecast. A gap is a very low occupancy day preceded and followed by days that are not considered low occupancy. The *stay-through* tactic intends to boost occupancy for the gap day(s) by promoting reservations that arrive before and check out after the gap day(s). If successful, this tactic generates revenue both from the extra days of reservations and from filling the gap.

Unfortunately, booking extra days may not necessarily fit the travel plans of potential guests. It is not unusual for trip planning to start by booking transportation, especially if it includes air travel. Once flight arrangements are finalized, most guests are not in a position to change flight dates on a whim, regardless of any incentives a hotel might offer. These circumstances can make it difficult for reservation agents to use the stay-through tactic effectively.

Close to Arrival

A revenue manager may choose to close a given day to arrivals if he or she believes that accepting more arrivals for that day would not benefit the hotel. After this measure is implemented, no more bookings would be accepted with an arrival on the closed day. Reasons for closing a day might include the arrival of one or more VIPs with extraordinary security arrangements (as is often the case with political figures, a famous rock band, a professional sports team, etc.) or renovating, deep cleaning, or redecorating floors or sections of a hotel. Or it could simply be a staffing and business flow decision. If the given day is both a high occupancy and high turnover day (that is, all or most of the rooms occupied the previous night will depart and all or most of the occupancy on the given day will come from new arrivals), a hotel with staffing constraints may decide at some point not to accept more bookings for the day in question. Suppose, for example, that the 350-room Rose Hotel expects 335 departures and 340 arrivals (40 individual transient guests and 300 conventioneers) on May 15. All 300 conventioneers need an in-room set-up with one of six different welcome packages corresponding to which of the six scheduled seminars they are attending. The guests will arrive as individuals from all over the world. Because the hotel believes it will have to stretch its resources to the limits to manage the turnover of 335 rooms and the arrival of the conventioneers, it decides to close the day for additional new arrivals. It believes that the revenue gained from selling its last ten rooms would probably not justify the added challenges those guests would represent. After this decision is made, all systems will display the same restriction, and no reservation agent will be authorized to override the arrival control measure. Hotel Rose is closed for arrival on May 15.

This tactic should be used with caution. The risks in applying this tactic are high. High-yield reservations (long-staying and full-rate-paying guests) or significant lifetime value guests may be turned away just because they picked the "wrong" arrival day. The revenue management thinking would suggest that the Hotel Rose in the above case should find a better way to deal with the operational challenges (such as giving both the housekeeping department and registration at the front desk additional resources). It will often be more beneficial to continue to accept bookings—possibly even overbooking and walking low-risk low-yield arrivals—and keep the reservations that are the most important revenue source of a hotel. Revenue managers need to be selective when they have options. Closing a date to arrival is seldom the best option for revenue maximization, though it can sometimes be an appropriate response to unusual situations.

Capacity Management

Capacity management is an essential revenue management tactic. Its objective is to maximize revenue through maximum guestroom occupancy on any given night. On nights when full occupancy seems attainable, most hotels do more than leave it to chance: they overbook the hotel. *Overbooking* means accepting more bookings for a given day than the hotel has the capacity to meet (such as a 400-room hotel accepting 405 bookings.) Before deciding to use this tactic, a hotel should look into its legality; in some jurisdictions, overbooking can be against the law. Some hotels choose never to use this tactic on principle, which a decision that deserves respect. However, the majority of transient hotels in urban commercial markets use overbooking to their advantage very successfully.

The rationale for this ambitious measure lies in the fact that every hotel deals with cancellations, no-shows, and early departures (understays). Hotels usually have more available rooms to work with than their bookings suggest, because a number of those bookings will never materialize. Moreover, that number is reasonably predictable based on historical trends. If a hotel's records show that 2 percent of its guests with reservations typically don't show up to check in (no-shows), 1 percent cancels before arrival, and 2 percent of guests who are scheduled to check out after the day in question will in fact check out early on or before that day, the hotel can make fairly safe estimates for forecasting purposes.

Note, however, that there are also some statistics that *reduce* room availability, such as overstays and out-of-order rooms. *Overstays* are people scheduled to check out on a given day who decide to stay longer.

The total effect of these elements is sometimes called the *wash factor*. The hotel "washes" its data to remove the misleading parts. The result helps the manager estimate how many units it would be safe to overbook on a given day. The accuracy of that projection is the key. Hotels that are comfortable using the tactic can maximize revenue on high occupancy days by preventing revenue loss from understays, no-shows, and cancellations.

However, using this tactic is not without risks. There will be days when things refuse to fall into place nicely. On a day when nobody cancels, everyone shows up, and no one checks out early, management has to deal with the consequences. Those are the nights when the front office will run out of rooms before it runs out of guests holding confirmed reservations. When this occurs, the front office staff must explain that the hotel cannot honor the reservation. The industry term for this is *walking a guest*. It is fairly standard practice for the hotel to help such guests secure alternate lodging. In North America, hotels usually will also pick up the room charge of guests who are walked, but this practice cannot be taken for granted in other markets. Local customs and supply/demand dynamics may differ a great deal.

In essence, revenue managers must decide whether they prefer to manage the risk of revenue loss or the risk of overbooking. The operational consequences of this capacity management tactic may put front office employees into very delicate situations. Fortunately, proven measures exist that help manage these situations.

When it is necessary to walk guests, the front office should book adequate quantity and quality nearby. No manager should walk a guest to a lower-rated hotel. The accommodating hotel should be of equivalent or greater service level or rating classification to mitigate the inconvenience and reduce the chance of further irritating the guest. It is common practice to schedule inexperienced staff for the evening shift, but on a night when the hotel expects to walk guests, inexperienced desk staff should never be left on their own. Managers don't want to see their hotel making the news for the wrong reason. Guests who are irate over a relocation gone bad can cause significant public relations damage. An experienced supervisor or an assistant front office manager should stay until the last walked guest is taken care of. Relocating a guest is a skill that can be perfected only through experience. Guest reactions to getting walked can be unpredictable.

One sometimes hears stories about disgruntled guests suing the hotels that walked them. Litigation has certainly been brought. However, there are no known cases of successful lawsuits against hotels for walking a guest. The existing litigation suggests that hotels should have a policy regarding walking and that under no circumstances should a hotel profit from it. Many hotels include a clause in their confirmation notes that mentions the possibility of overbooking and how it would be handled in order to create awareness regarding this possibility. A common stumbling block for litigants has been that they are unable to show that the breach of the contract (the reservation) led them to suffer specific consequences, especially when the hotel offered to help find alternate lodging and to pay for it.

Preventive Measures

Managers must try to prevent overstays on critical days. It is wise to flag the folio of those guests whose departure plans are suspect and get a commitment to an exact departure date. To communicate and ensure a definite departure date, front desks may require registering guests to initial their departure date on the registration card at arrival, especially if that date is overbooked. It never hurts to get things in writing.

Some guests may genuinely not know at check-in how long they will stay. Others may fail to inform the front office if their plans change. When overbooking is involved, it is up to the front office manager to track down the in-house guests and clearly state how long the hotel can accommodate them.

Consider the situation carefully if guests scheduled to check out on an overbooked day decide they want to extend their stay. Can a guest decide to stay one more night than indicated at arrival? Absolutely. It happens all the time. Can the guest do that without the hotel's approval? Absolutely *not*. Both parties to a contract (written or oral) must agree to any modifications. A rate and a departure date are vital parts in the simple contract that is established between hotel and guest. Hotel managers are on solid legal ground to deny any extensions as long as their actions are reasonable. It often helps to explain the situation and to offer options.

Again, management must decide whether it prefers dealing with an unhappy guest whose extension request is denied or with an unhappy guest arriving with reservation in hand who will have to be walked. The deliberation deserves thought. If there is one revenue management rule to apply in this situation, it would simply be that the business of a known return guest should not be jeopardized for the business of an unknown guest. Revenue management thinking suggests that a high lifetime value customer is just too important to risk losing in order to accommodate an unknown guest that may never return. With that in mind, the decisions should always be handled on a case-by-case basis.

If guests must be walked, the decision of *which* guests to walk must be addressed. The winnowing can start by identifying those reservations the hotel would definitely *not* like to walk under any circumstances. There are the VIPs, frequent-stay club members, honeymooners, special requests, multi-night stays, and others who would not make good candidates for relocation. Guests who get walked are usually (but not exclusively) the very late arrivals. Because of the time of day, single female travelers and business travelers generally are not the best candidates to be walked. With corporate travelers, there may be a lot more riding on the decision than one arrival; the whole corporate account can be at risk if the hotel walks the wrong corporate guest. Single-night arrivals with no history and leisure guests who don't mind the apology coupled with a complimentary night elsewhere may make better potential candidates for walking.

Reclaiming Rooms

Revenue managers, front office managers, and executive housekeepers must work together to anticipate the days when a hotel may run short of rooms. With effective cooperation, a hotel might "find" enough usable rooms to significantly reduce the number of guests who must be walked. This can make a tremendous difference.

Selling the Couch

This is a true story of a guest who got an unusual accommodation one night instead of getting walked. It happened in the Hotel Béke in Budapest, close to one of the major railway stations. Mr. B. was a regular guest at the Béke. He was a purchaser for a small company and didn't know his way around the big city. He came once or twice a month, stayed always one night, and he wasn't picky; any room would do. After a number of years, he had earned the status of a regular guest and stopped making advance bookings. He just showed up, accepted any room, and never made a fuss.

On a night when the hotel was heavily overbooked, Mr. B. walked in and matter-of-factly inquired which room could be his for the night. He was flabbergasted to learn that not one room was available. As acceptance of this bad news sank in, he suggested he would just find an armchair in a quiet corner of the lobby and spend the night right there. After all, he had a 6:15 train to catch the next morning.

This gave an idea to the desk clerk, who was genuinely sorry to deny accommodation to such a loyal guest. The clerk knew there was a couch on the top guest floor in the small lobby in front of the elevator. He asked Mr. B. to come back around midnight, after things had quieted down. He would have housekeeping make a bed on that couch for Mr. B., who gladly accepted the offer.

Some early-rising guests the next morning called anxiously to report the man occupying the couch of the elevator lobby on the top floor, but other than that, everything worked out fine. Mr. B. was charged the price of an extra bed, which he settled, leaving the usual tip for the staff. When the front office manager showed up, he asked whether the previous night was a full house. The night clerk said, "Boss, we had record occupancy. We even sold the couch in the top floor elevator lobby."

Experienced hotel managers know that additional guestrooms for the night can often be found by looking hard enough. The first step is to compare the daily housekeeping report, which is based on a physical inspection of each guestroom at around check-out time, to the room status in the computerized property management system (PMS). It is not unusual for the front office and housekeeping to have different room statuses for the same room. If the PMS shows a given room as occupied, but housekeeping reports no luggage or other trace of occupancy, the discrepancy must be resolved.

Out-of-order (OOO) rooms should also be considered on sold-out days. The reason code (if there is one) is important in determining whether the OOO status could be changed. Some rooms may have been taken out of service for scheduled maintenance work or deep cleaning. Others may have been placed out of order because of minor defects. If a room can be assigned to a new arrival, even at a reduced rate, it makes sense to put it back in inventory instead of walking a guest. Housekeeping and engineering staff know the rooms best, so the front office needs to work with them closely. Peeling wallpaper, a torn shower curtain, or a bad carpet stain may be temporarily covered up or acknowledged by a discount if that's what it takes to prevent a walk.

Function Rooms. Some hotels have small boardrooms or executive conference rooms that could be temporarily set up for one-night stays. If these rooms have a washroom and a pull-out sofa, or if a cot or rollaway can be placed in the room, some guests may accept them for one night in exchange for a reduced room rate, a complimentary meal voucher, or other incentives. Most local health and safety regulations will require that each "temporary room" be equipped with its own toilet facilities, television set, telephone, and door with its own locking mechanism.

Parloring. If a hotel has suites where the connecting door between the parlor (sitting room) and bedroom(s) can be locked and each room has separate entrances from the hallway with locks, these units can be sold separately if the rooms have televisions, telephones, and adjoining bathrooms. Volunteers can be offered a special deal at arrival. The room also needs a pull-out sofa, Murphy bed or a rollaway to be offered to volunteers at a reduced rate.

Upgrading. A useful tactic is to offer an upgrade if the hotel is oversold for a particular room type. An upgrade to a junior suite can help satisfy a guest when the hotel is short of the non-smoking queen room originally booked. If three single reservations turn out to be three colleagues checking in at the same time, a quick-thinking guest service agent can offer an upgrade into a single multi-bedroom suite in exchange for their separate standard accommodations. The offer of a bottle of a fine drink may sweeten the deal and allow the hotel can get back three rooms.

Displacement Analysis

Group revenue can be a significant contributor to rooms division revenue for most hotels in urban commercial markets. Management must determine the ideal capacity and rate allocation dedicated to the group market in any given period. The targeted market mix will be determined based on the hotel's strategy. These considerations are certainly subject to seasonality. A hotel may more aggressively pursue the group segment in shoulder seasons and off-seasons than in the main season, when it caters more to transient guests. A hotel's historical data provides a good source of information about the staying and booking patterns of each market segment.

Who are the most important partners of a hotel that relies on group business to achieve its revenue potential? The list includes tour operators, travel agents, convention and visitor bureaus, global distribution systems, meeting planners, and a variety of associations to start with. There will be times when a hotel needs its partners to fill gaps or boost the occupancy in low-demand periods. Sometimes, it is the other way around: the groups may be in desperate need to find accommodation when overall demand is high. Supply/demand dynamics have a tendency to fluctuate due to the cycles of the economy (between prosperity and recession) and changes in seasonality (from peak to shoulder to off-season). Revenue managers and sales directors have learned to appreciate the significance of good working relationships with key group clients and know too well that group business cannot be ignored. If a hotel would like to benefit from group revenue when overall demand is soft, groups need to be accommodated also when overall demand is strong.

Industry Insight: Overbooking

By Julian Darisse, Shangri-La Hotels & Resorts

Depending on how you feel about overbooking, I've had the opportunity or misfortune of dealing with upset guests, supporting under-pressure staff, and nights as Night Manager when 5:00 A.M. couldn't come soon enough.

My first experience with overbooking came in Toronto at Canada's largest hotel with 1590 rooms, the Delta Chelsea Hotel. The Chelsea is a centrally-located four-star hotel with a massive lobby with lots of activity. It wasn't uncommon to have 800 check-outs and 900 check-ins on a given day. As I gained more experience on reception, they would assign me to the Status Control Supervisor position on late shift. This meant that I would assist my colleagues with assigning rooms and would often decide whether or not to upgrade or downgrade a guest. I treated this situation like a jigsaw puzzle, having to put the right guests into the right rooms to make a perfect fit.

I remember one day in September 2002 when we went as far as –30 (on rooms). We had parlor rooms (which weren't included in our 1590 rooms inventory) that had everything normal rooms have (except for a pullout bed) that we used to increase our standard rooms inventory. With my front office manager's consent, I started to select guests that I felt would take these rooms: single travelers, one-nighters, guests in their twenties. I sold at least ten rooms by lowering their rate; the guests benefit by saving money, housekeeping still prepares their room as normal and they still have all room amenities, except for a standard bed. We further washed about five tentative bookings and had a further ten pre-registration bookings to "play with"; pre-registration bookings are good to load up on in an overbooking situation, because you can fill them if necessary with current-day guests or pre-register the original guest. By 7:00 P.M., we were about –5; by the end of the night, we had a perfect fill with five no-shows.

Working in London at the Langham Hotel, I had to walk guests to other hotels, making sure to avoid high-yield and regular guests. It occasionally happened that we had a large group that couldn't get their connecting flight out through Heathrow, or an unexpected storm delayed train travelers from going home or we had a technical fault somewhere in the hotel.

Be careful with the last reason for an overbooking! When one of my colleagues claimed that we had a bad flood, one of our walked guests asked to see the flood; luckily, a guest had fallen asleep and flooded their bathtub and room with water! I try to avoid saying that we are "overbooked" or "sold out"; both are clichés and can upset clients even more, so I tend to employ "we're fully committed," which seems to go over better.

London was also great for the "call around"; keeping in touch with other area duty managers and night managers creates an industry camaraderie and letting each other know how "deep" you are on a sold-out night will garner good future relations. In fact, if our hotel was close to filling, I would contact a few of our competitors to let them know that we had a couple of rooms left if they needed help. More often than not, they would take the offer when oversold.

Industry Insight *(continued)*

One thing to keep in mind is that the rate that you charge a competitor hotel for a walk will more than likely dictate what rate they will charge you in future, so remember to be fair.

Knowing which hotels have how many rooms is important for night managers because they are the last in command at the end of the night; this information should be gathered by the reservations manager, revenue manager, front office manager, or late duty manager. That's the least they can do before going to the pub.

Capacity management is ultimately about teamwork, because it takes colleagues from various departments and areas to make sure guests are happy and that the hotel is generating revenue.

Hotels will sometimes turn away transient business able and willing to pay higher room rates in order to allocate inventory to groups at lower rates instead. Can this decision be consistent with revenue maximization strategies? In the right circumstances, a *displacement analysis* can determine the quantifiable benefits of different options.

A displacement analysis is not always appropriate. If a hotel has unsold capacity and reliable forecasting indicates little chance of selling that block of rooms, the hotel is happy to book anything at all. In this case, it doesn't make sense to conduct a displacement analysis for a group booking. In a soft market where a hotel is delighted to get any group business, no displacement will likely take place. However, when demand is high, the revenue manager will likely have to qualify and rank bookings, then select from among potential customers. A displacement analysis should be completed if the acceptance of a group booking will result in turning away other business (transient or other groups). In such a situation, the displacement analysis is a useful and efficient tool that helps a hotel determine which booking to accept.

A hotel may use a spreadsheet-based system to compute the variables. The temptation is significant to produce a quick "yes" or "no" answer to a request. But the numeric results of the analysis should not be the only criteria for the decision. Although revenue management is a numbers-driven process, it should never be reduced simply to a push/pull game with dollar figures. It is the *interpretation* of the numbers and all other relevant factors that should drive the revenue management tactics selected.

Why is it necessary to conduct a numeric analysis when management may end up favoring a customer that would pay lower room rates? Here are some considerations:

- Other revenue streams (food and beverage, function rooms, etc.) need to be considered as well to calculate the total revenue impact.
- The lifetime business value of a group client may be an important variable.

- Management needs to know the difference in profitability between scenarios to plan and budget effectively.
- Market share, revenue mix, and other strategic objectives may play a role.

Displacement analysis is a four-step process: (1) Establish net room revenue differential; (2) Establish the net food and beverage revenue differential; (3) Determine other revenue; and (4) Summarize. It compares the net revenue differential between scenarios.

In order to calculate net room revenue, the variable costs need to be identified and subtracted from the room rate. In some cases, fees payable per reservation (as a percentage of room revenue and/or a fixed amount per booking) must also be subtracted from the room rate. Other relevant fees may include a percentage of room revenue for marketing and royalty due under a franchise agreement. Some contracts secure a central reservation office (CRO) or a call center fee per booking. Assume the following:

Transient room rate:	$150
Variable cost:	18
Franchise fee of 8%: $150 × 0.08	12
CRO if applicable:	6

In this case, net room revenue is $150 – ($18.00 + $12.00 + $6.00), or $114.00.

In order to establish the net room revenue differential, the following variables need to be known:

- The number of group room nights
- Group room rate
- Group room revenue
- Net group room revenue
- The number of displaced transient room nights
- Displaced room rate
- Displaced room revenue
- Displaced net room revenue
- Difference between net group room revenue and net displaced room revenue.

The comparison of net group room revenue and net displaced room revenue will produce the net room revenue differential. Let's look at an example.

The Windsor has 400 rooms. The average transient rate in March is $142 and the variable room cost is $17. The Windsor is affiliated with a franchisor that charges a royalty fee of 4 percent and a marketing fee of 3 percent. The combined fees are applicable to room revenue. The local university's business student alumni association plans a reunion. The group requests single rooms for $65 per room night, meals (breakfast for $10, lunch for $24 dinner for $32), and other services for a three-day event between March 6–8 as follows:

Date	Rooms	Breakfast	Lunch	Dinner	Meeting Room
March 6	85	85	0	85	—
March 7	80	80	0	0	$300
March 8	70	70	40	0	$300
Total	235	235	40	85	$600

The organizer of the Alumni Association believes that 70 percent of the group members will purchase one beverage per day. The revenue manager of the Windsor would like to conduct a displacement analysis before confirming or rejecting the group's request.

The forecasted occupancy of the hotel for the days in question is as follows:

March 6	March 7	March 8
365	360	310

Note that the Windsor can accept the group only if it displaces some of the forecasted transient demand. If the group takes 85 rooms on March 6, that will leave only 315 rooms for transient guests, which is 50 fewer rooms than the amount forecasted. March 7 will have 40 fewer rooms than the forecasted transient demand.

An initial comparison shows the transient room cost as $17 + ($142 × 7%), or $26.94, and the group room cost as $17.00 + ($65 × 7%), or $21.55.

The hotel's capture rate (the percentage of transient guests purchasing a meal) and other relevant data per meal period for transient guests in March is:

Meal	Price	Food Cost %	Food Cost*	Net Revenue	Transient Capture %
Breakfast	$12	30%	$3.60	$8.40	70%
Lunch	$28	34%	$9.52	$18.48	20%
Dinner	$40	32%	$12.80	$27.20	40%

*Cost of ingredients

The group meals will be calculated with the same food costs per item at discounted prices: $10 for breakfast, $24 for lunch, and $32 for dinner.

Group Meal	Breakfast	Lunch	Dinner
Price	$10.00	$24.00	$32.00
Food cost	$3.60	$9.52	$12.80

Beverage costs and prices are the same for group guests and transients. The beverage capture rate of transient guests in the Windsor is 40 percent. The average beverage price is $6.00 and the average beverage cost is 29 percent, so the variable beverage cost is $1.74.

We establish the net room revenue differential as follows:

The number of group room nights:	235	
Group room rate:	$65	
Group room revenue:	$15,275	(235 × $65)
Group room cost:	$21.55	($17 + [$65 × 7%])
Net group room revenue/room:	$43.45	($65 − $21.55)
Total net group room revenue:	$10,210.75	(235 × $43.45)

The displaced transient room nights:	90	
Displaced room rate:	$142	
Displaced room revenue:	$12,780	(90 × $142)
Transient room cost:	$26.94	($17 + [$142 × 7%])
Net displaced room revenue/room:	$115.06	($142 − $26.94)
Total displaced net room revenue:	$10,355.40	(90 × $115.06)

The room revenue analysis shows that accepting the group will result in a net room revenue decrease of $144.65.

We establish the net food and beverage revenue differential in much the same way, working with each revenue source separately. Recall that beverage costs and prices are no different for groups and transients at the Windsor.

Average beverage margin:	$4.26	
Total group room nights:	235	
Group beverage capture rate:	70%	
Total beverage contribution from group:	$700.77	($4.26 × 235 × 70%)

Displaced transient room nights:	90	
Transient beverage capture rate:	40%	
Total displaced beverage contribution:	$153.36	($4.26 × 90 × 40%)

Accepting the group results in a beverage contribution increase of $700.77 − $153.36, or $547.41. Turning to food, we determine the following:

Group breakfasts:	235	
Breakfast price for group:	$10	
Breakfast cost:	$3.60	
Margin on group breakfast:	$6.40	
Group breakfast contribution:	$1,504.00	(235 × $6.40)
Group lunches:	40	
Lunch price for group:	$24.00	
Lunch cost:	$9.52	
Margin on group lunch:	$14.48	
Group lunch contribution:	$579.20	(40 × $14.48)
Group dinners:	85	
Dinner price for group:	$32.00	
Dinner cost:	$12.80	
Margin on group dinner:	$19.20	
Group dinner contribution:	$1,632.00	(85 × $19.20)
Total group food contribution:	$3,715.20	($1,504 + $579.20 + $1,632)

Displaced transient room nights:	90	
Transient breakfast price:	$12.00	
Breakfast cost:	$3.60	
Margin on transient breakfast:	$8.40	
Transient breakfast capture rate:	70%	
Displaced transient breakfast contribution:	$529.20	(90 × 70% × $8.40)
Transient lunch price:	$28.00	
Lunch cost:	$9.52	
Margin on transient lunch:	$18.48	
Transient lunch capture rate:	20%	
Displaced transient lunch contribution:	$332.64	(90 × 20% × $18.48)
Transient dinner price:	$40.00	
Dinner cost:	$12.80	
Margin on transient dinner:	$27.20	
Transient dinner capture rate:	40%	
Displaced transient dinner contribution:	$979.20	(90 × 40% × $27.20)
Total displaced transient food contribution:	$1,841.04	($529.20 + $332.64 + $979.20)

Accepting the group results in a food contribution increase of $3,715.20 – $1,841.04, or $1,874.16 from all three meal periods.

The combined food and beverage net revenue differential is $1,874.16 + $547.41, or $2,421.51.

The third step is to determine any other revenue. In this case, the group wants to rent a meeting room for two days, generating total other revenue of $600.

The final step is to summarize the results. Doing so reveals the following:

Net room revenue differential:	($144.65)
Beverage contribution differential:	$547.41
Food contribution differential:	$1,874.16
Other revenue contribution:	$600
Total increase from group:	$2,876.92

Accepting the group results in an overall net revenue gain of $2,876.92, which is a combination of a decrease in net room revenue and increases in net food, beverage and other revenue streams.

This displacement analysis shows that accepting the group will increase the hotel's profitability for the days in question, though it will come at the cost of some transient business. Management may choose to accept the group after this analysis, or it may consider other potential options based on the market conditions and the hotel's strategic objectives. For example, can the hotel persuade the group to accept alternative dates that will not displace transient business? The displacement analysis results do not dictate a simple answer, but they give management critical information it will need to make an informed decision.

The calculations of displacement analysis can be automated by installing formulas in a spreadsheet template. This tool can speed up the decision-making process and make it easier to compare different bookings at varying price points.

Endnotes

1. Yesawich, Pepperdine, Brown, and Russel, *National Travel Monitor 2003*. Presented at the International Hotel, Motel & Restaurant Show, New York, N.Y., November 2005.
2. Yesawich et al.
3. Cathy A. Enz, Linda Canina, and Mark Lomanno, "Why Discounting Doesn't Work: The Dynamics of Rising Occupancy and Falling Revenue Among Competitors," *CHR Reports* 4, no. 7 (2004). Available at www.hotelschool.cornell.edu/research/chr/pubs/reports/abstract-13599.html.
4. Linda Canina and Steven Carvell, "Lodging Demand for Urban Hotels in Major Metropolitan Markets," *CHR Reports* 3, no. 3 (2003). Available at www.hotelschool.cornell.edu/research/chr/pubs/reports/abstract-13608.html.
5. Yesawich et al.
6. Linda Canina and Cathy A. Enz, "Revenue Management in U.S. Hotels: 2001-2005," *CHR Reports* 6, no. 8 (2006). Available at www.hotelschool.cornell.edu/research/chr/pubs/reports/abstract-14021.html.

References

Canina, Linda, and Cathy A. Enz, "Why Discounting Still Doesn't Work: A Hotel Pricing Update," *CHR Reports* 6, no. 2 (2006).

Enz, Cathy A. "Hotel Pricing in a Networked World." *Cornell Hotel and Restaurant Administration Quarterly* 44, no. 1 (2003).

Enz, Cathy A., and Linda Canina. "An Examination of Revenue Management in Relation to Hotels' Pricing Strategies." *CHR Reports* 5, no. 6 (2005).

Chapter 4 Outline

Competencies

1. Describe the role that differentiation plays in demand generation and the most frequently used differentiation strategies. (pp. 65–69)
2. Identify and describe several marketing concepts that play a significant role in strategic revenue management efforts. (pp. 69–77)
3. Outline critical considerations involved in strategic pricing decisions. (pp. 77–80)
4. Describe the nature and significance of revenue streams management. (pp. 80–81)
5. Explain the nature, process, and purposes of creating packaged products. (pp. 81–86)
6. Identify and describe various distribution methods and channels and explain why distribution channel management is important to a hotel's success. (pp. 86–91)

4

Strategic Revenue Management

MANY REVENUE MANAGERS can skillfully use tactical measures to improve revenue generation in the short term. Such managers may well "hit a home run" once in a while. But in order to truly maximize revenue in a coherent and effective way over the long term, revenue managers must move beyond short-term tactics to embrace long-term strategic planning. Tactics are most effective when they support an overarching strategic goal. The proof of this is in the results. Hotels that use only revenue management tactics are not as consistently successful as hotels that use such tactics in support of a clear strategic goal. Hotels are long-term capital investments by nature. They have the ability to use revenue management as a strategic tool to help lay the foundations of sustainable success.

The integration of tactical and strategic revenue management helps management generate demand with proven marketing measures. The strategic approach sees pricing in the larger context of desired target markets, rather than as a nightly race to the highest possible revenue. Strategic revenue management topics also include the overall management of all a hotel's revenue streams, as well as strategic packaging and distribution channel management.

These topics are complex and exciting because it is at the strategic level where true success can be secured. Revenue managers who recognize and apply the full arsenal of strategic revenue management are able to handle any challenges offered by a dynamic marketplace. Using strategy as a guide, the best managers find optimum solutions under any set of circumstances.

Demand Generation

The objective of demand generation is to produce the most possible revenue under any supply/demand conditions. In order to achieve this, strategic revenue management goes beyond the management of existing demand to manipulate and increase demand. Using demand generation strategies, revenue managers can take a proactive rather than reactive approach to maximizing revenue.

Supply/demand dynamics are driven primarily by market forces. A hotel can influence demand because it is an active player in its market. Revenue managers have a significant role in helping the members of chosen market segments to become guests of their hotels. They do this in part through product development and careful product positioning among the comparable options available to potential guests.

Ambitious hotels want their voices to stand out and be heard by targeted customers against the noise of the market. The market noise is loud and constant, as customers get bombarded by advertisements and marketing appeals of all sorts. A hotel's marketing budget is limited even in good times, and marketing managers can work only with the value proposition of a given hotel, branded or not. At the very heart of even the most creative marketing appeal, there must be a marketable product. One of the key drivers of marketability is differentiation.

Differentiation

A hotel can differentiate itself from its competitors in more meaningful ways than room rate. Two examples of successful hotel brands that got started in the early 1960s in North America illustrate the theory quite well. La Quinta Inns championed a concept called limited service by offering hotels without restaurants and catering to the needs of budget-conscious business travelers by placing the telephone on a desk rather than beside the bed. This helped those who needed the telephone for business purposes. The other example is Four Seasons Hotels, which was the first luxury chain in North America to offer concierges, complementary overnight shoe shines, 24-hour room service, bathrobes, and shampoo in their hotels at premium rates. Both brands became successful by differentiating their products and grew to become significant players in their fields over the years.

The success of differentiation is in eye of the guest. A feature needs to be more than simply different. Guests need to value the feature for differentiation based on that feature to work. For example, it might make little sense for an all-inclusive resort hotel to offer no-charge faxing and photocopying as a differentiating feature, because this feature would probably not be relevant to vacationing leisure guests. On the other hand, a hotel offering "one-minute check-in after 3 P.M. or the night is free" to loyalty program members might find that its time-pressed business travelers highly value this feature.

The most frequently applied differentiation strategies build on unique features, level of service, location, and brand affiliation.

Unique Features. If a hotel has a unique feature that can be successfully exploited to differentiate it, marketing communications can be built around that feature. Some hotels can be considered one-of-a-kind because of their unique locations or architecture, such as historic hotels converted from ancient buildings (castles, chateaux, palaces, monasteries, manors, etc.), underwater hotels, ice hotels, atrium hotels, and hotels on any theme from an Egyptian pyramid to Venetian lagoons to rock and roll.

If the hotel is not unique as a building, it may still develop unique amenities. A hotel may have the largest water slide in town or the only ice skating rink in a desert location. It may be the only hotel inside a baseball stadium with a field view or the place with the most famous musical dancing fountains, the best gym, or the smartest and fastest elevators. Any of these could be a unique selling point. Several years ago, Starwood Hotels and Resorts upgraded essential amenities to gain successful differentiation. This multi-brand corporation began its campaign after a commissioned sleep study concluded that many guests have unsatisfactory sleep experiences in hotels. Starwood launched the Heavenly Bed—top-quality mattresses and bedding upgrades—at its Westin Hotels brand. The successful differentiation led to similar initiatives at other Starwood brands (such as the Sweet Sleeper at Sheraton).

Some landmark hotels are so famous and prestigious that even a brand affiliation essentially becomes a subtitle (The Waldorf=Astoria New York, managed by Hilton, or The Savoy in London, managed by Fairmont, are such properties). The cachet of the name a landmark hotel has successfully established over the years can eclipse everything else. That can be the best source of differentiation, but it is also the hardest to earn.

Any unique feature not provided by default (like a location or architecture) can be difficult to earn, but once established, it can be the source of competitive advantage for years to come. Any hotel that can claim a unique feature is in a strong position to build on its unique value proposition through premium pricing and a high level of awareness that helps generate and sustain demand.

Level of Service. An extraordinary level of service can also be a differentiator. For example, some hotel chains have built a culture of service excellence. The challenges are significant. The approach to business must incorporate every facet of operations, from hiring to supply chain management. A high employee-to-guest ratio is one piece of the puzzle. Detailed attention must be given to the thread count of the chosen linens, the angle of pen placement on the note pad, the temperature settings in guestrooms, and the maximum number of rings allowed when answering a call. In every guestroom, consistent quality must be delivered every day. Individualized "high touch" services are offered, and empowered employees never settle for a compromise in the pursuit of perfection, whether it concerns a meal, a floral arrangement, or a last-minute ticket request for a sold-out event.

Service-related differentiation may not always be so resource-intensive. Pet-friendly hotels offer a service that typically does not require extensive investment, even when providing special menu and room service for pets. This differentiation can matter a great deal to some market segments.

There is an emerging category classified as *select service* that is somewhere between full service and limited service. The intended differentiation targets business travelers who may not need the whole range of services offered by a traditional full-service hotel, but who need more services than a limited-service hotel traditionally offers. This service category offers value for the traveler through hip design, high-end technological amenities, and selected food and beverage service to meet the needs of emerging customer segments. These brands (for example, Four Points by Sheraton, Holiday Inn Express, Element and Aloft from Starwood) in many cases use the halo of a well-established "mother ship" brand. The lower investment requirements help to take certain brands down-market and make them feasible options for interested franchisees. In smaller markets where a full-service hotel is not financially viable, a select-service operation with streamlined food and beverage services may be the best fit.

Location. A prime or unique location can provide a highly valuable point of differentiation in markets with high barriers to entry. The airport hotel inside the terminal building, the closest hotel to a main attraction (festival site, museum, theme park, etc.), the best ocean front among other resort hotels, and the hotel right on the slopes at a ski resort will (other things being equal) generate higher revenue than competitors in less favorable locations.

As many hotels have learned over the years, the factors that determine whether a location is prime or not can change over time. Many one-time prime locations have become secondary over time for a variety of reasons. Hotels built near railway stations in the heart of a city have often suffered when the station relocated. For that matter, hotels near railway stations also lost a lot of their business when people began to travel primarily by automobile. U.S. hotels on important roads through towns and cities lost a lot of their business when the interstate highway system begun in the 1950s bypassed them and traffic volume dropped deeply on what came to be considered the old country roads. A fine seashore resort can be badly damaged by hurricanes, or a city famous for top-notch entertainment and fine cuisine can lose its market position as a favored destination after a tragic flood, as the industry has witnessed in New Orleans. These examples are humbling reminders that even the advantage of a prime location cannot be taken for granted.

Some locations offer such unique differentiation that a hotel can become an attraction in itself. Examples include under the sea in Dubai; high on the cliff wall of an ancient volcano on the Greek island of Santorini; deep in the Canadian wilderness on a lake accessible only by float plane; on a tiny private coral island in the Maldives; in the heart of Paris just steps away from the sights; or right on Times Square in New York City. These locations offer the highest barriers to entry for any possible competitor.

Brand Affiliation. A brand name can help a hotel differentiate itself from competitors. A successful brand can be the source of quantifiable competitive advantages. Most branded properties outperform non-branded ones as a result of premium pricing and efficient central reservation systems. Brands tend to have more resources for promotions and for efficiently managing their distribution channels. As the commercial lodging industry is a very competitive one, successful brands can be significant factors in revenue maximization. The brand recognition a flag can bring to a hotel will help the guest know what to expect in terms of price level, service quality, amenities, and other product attributes.

Branding is prevalent in the lodging industry. Single- and multi-brand hotel companies capitalize on this marketing trend and continually create new brands to cater to changing lifestyles and consumer preferences. Some brands own and operate their properties, but franchising and management contracts have become the preferred methods of brand growth. Under both the franchising and management contract business models, revenue generation is the key source of financial viability. As a result, revenue management has become mission critical for each stakeholder.

For hotel property owners who consider acquiring a brand through franchising, the main considerations are the advantages gained through brand recognition and the sales and marketing support a brand would deliver.

For property owners seeking a qualified manager to run the hotel, the main consideration is creating a management contract that aligns the interests of owners and managers. In the earlier days of management contracts, the contracts often favored the management company. By the 1990s, owners and their representatives (known as *asset managers*) began to effectively negotiate contracts in a way that better aligned the parties' interests. Some management companies (known as *first-tier* or *branded* management contract companies) offer a brand of their own, while others (known as *second-tier* or *unbranded* management contract companies) may manage properties under many flags. First-tier companies offer the power of their recognized brand, efficiencies on the cost side based on their supply chain management systems and volume discounts, and impressive revenue potential through multi-channel distribution systems. Second-tier companies can't provide the added benefit of a proven hotel brand, so hiring them will not produce any extra cachet that could translate into premium rates, but an owner may have more negotiating power and can exert more influence on balance. Owners who hire second-tier management contract companies may also decide to purchase a franchise or to use other branding options, such as referral organizations or marketing alliances (Best Western Hotels, Leading Hotels of the World, Relais & Chateaux, Small Luxury Hotels of the World, etc.).

Brand penetration in the hotel industry varies significantly on a global scale. In the United States, more than 70 percent of the hotels are branded. In Canada, the ratio is around 40 percent. France has the highest brand penetration in Europe, where about 25 percent of hotels are flagged.

Marketing Strategies for Revenue Management

Marketing is closely related to most facets of revenue management. Revenue management does not teach (or re-teach) the discipline of marketing, but it builds on most elements of marketing and discusses some of them from the perspective of revenue optimization.

Market Segmentation Methods

If a company believes that everyone is a potential customer, a mass marketing approach is reasonable. However, the hotel industry has realized that the market it serves is not homogeneous. In order to better understand the characteristics of different people, the market can be divided into groups that have common needs and distinct buying habits. Market segmentation is a necessary strategic measure for best results. Major traditional market segmentation variables are geographic, demographic, psychographic, and behavioral traits and price-sensitivity.

Geographic segmentation can be as broad or as narrow as necessary. There are geographic information systems (GISs) that contain significant amounts of information in databases that can be mined and layered based on numerous search criteria. Geographic areas can be identified by postal code or by geo-position (longitude and latitude) if that makes sense. It is frequently practical to use a location-based segmentation that considers driving distance to a destination. If one hotel considers a primary target market to be less than three hours' driving distance away, the boundaries of that geographic market can be identified on a map fairly simply.

Demographic segmentation includes age cohort, gender, nationality, marital status, family size, income bracket, and other similar information based on census data. One of the most frequently used terms in demographic segmentation is *Baby Boomers*. This age cohort includes those born between 1946–1964 in the United States, Canada, the United Kingdom, and Australia, where a significant spike occurred in birth rates after World War II. This cohort is large and affluent and is the target of a great number of marketing appeals.

Psychographic segmentation considers social class, lifestyle, and personality. The largest single group of customers (one third of the total) can be characterized as the mainstream group, made up of moderate income families that value security, avoid risk taking, like safety, and need social approval.

Behavioral segmentation's typical breakdown includes buying habits, attitudes toward a product, and usage rate, among other criteria. For example, the psychographic segment known as mainstreamers prefers a simple and uncomplicated way in every aspect of booking, arrival, and staying (behavioral) at a hotel. Family holidays and the need to feel comfortable in a foreign environment are important to them. The Holiday Inn brand hit the right button for this segment with an ad campaign that used the tag line, "The best surprise is no surprise at all." This carefully targeted promotion appealed to a specific segment that became the bread and butter of a hotel chain. If a marketing appeal combined more than one segmentation method and targeted domestic mainstreamers of a certain age bracket, it would be classified as psycho-demographic plus geographic segmentation.

A market segment can be any size that makes business sense. The most important aspect is that the group members need enough characteristics in common that they will respond in a similar way to a marketing appeal.

Segmentation can start on a broad basis and then be further refined with additional criteria if it makes sense. For example, we might start with the segment of corporate hotel guests that are domestic. If useful, we could further refine this segment to females who travel alone. Should there be a need for even further segmentation and reliable data is available, we might narrow the group to same state/province single female corporate travelers who have an annual income between $60,000–$99,000 and stay at least three times per year at a given hotel. This example combines geographic, demographic, and behavioral criteria.

Revenue managers also are keenly interested in distinguishing price-sensitive guests from those who are not price-sensitive. These two basic groups call for different marketing and revenue management approaches. A widely used measure of price-sensitivity is known as *elasticity*, sometimes called demand elasticity or price elasticity. Elasticity is a ratio that expresses how a change in the price of a product or service affects unit demand for that product or service. For hotel rooms, it is calculated as follows:

$$\text{Elasticity} = \frac{\text{Percent change in demand (unit occupancy)}}{\text{Percent change in room rate}}$$

The original unit demand and price are the bases on which the percentages are derived. That is, if a hotel changes an $80 room rate by $20 (to either $60 or $100), the percentage change is the dollar change divided by the original price, in this case, $20 ÷ $80, or 25 percent.

The concept of elasticity is based on the economic principle that, for a given level of demand in a market, a rise in price will cause unit sales to drop, while a drop in price will cause unit sales to rise. Elasticity tells us which change is larger. A value of less than 1.0 is interpreted as inelastic demand, while a value equal to or greater than 1.0 is interpreted as elastic demand.

This is important information to calculate and track because revenue managers want to know how customers will react to price changes. If a 5 percent price increase produces only a 2 percent drop in unit demand, the elasticity is 2 percent divided by 5 percent, or 0.4, which is inelastic. In this case, demand is such that a price increase will not reduce unit sales disproportionately. Stated another way, the market will bear the increase and the hotel's room revenues will increase. On the other hand, if the same 5 percent price increase produced a 10 percent drop in unit sales, the elasticity would be 10 percent divided by 5 percent, or 2.0, which is elastic. In this case, the price increase caused an even larger drop in sales, meaning that the hotel's room revenues will suffer.

Managers should examine elasticity especially when considering room discounting. Recall that in 2003, research conducted on 480 hotels revealed that, on average, for every 10 percent drop in room rate, demand rose by only 1.3 percent.[1] When demand is inelastic, room rate decreases will reduce total room revenue.

Different market segments display different levels of price elasticity. If a 5 percent room rate increase results in a 4 percent decrease from corporate bookings and a 12 percent decrease from leisure traveler bookings, the corporate segment was inelastic at 0.8, but the leisure segment's reaction was very elastic at 2.4.

Price sensitivity quantified with an elasticity index is a useful tool for tracking and benchmarking. Other frequently used elasticity indexes are income elasticity (which measures the change in income level compared with the change in quantity sold) and cross elasticity (which measures the price change of one product and compares it to the rate of change in sales of another product, such as the impact of a change in airfare on hotel bookings).

A New Segment: "M Commerce." Travelers are increasingly using mobile telecommunications technology for data access when traveling. Mobile users can easily get real-time price comparisons. Service providers use location-based triggers and global positioning system–based dynamic maps combined with access to online content regarding places of interest for travelers on the road. For example, Kootenay Rockies Tourism, a Canadian destination marketing organization, offers full online travel information services to mobile users. KootenayRockies.mobi provides travelers with hundreds of pages of information about accommodation options, attractions, events, and even restaurant menus, all of which is available through mobile phones or other handheld devices.[2]

The hotel industry is learning to pay attention to the so-called "road warriors"—frequent guests who purchase a significant amount of room nights in hotels while traveling on business. For revenue management purposes, it is important to note that these guests want quick, easy access to booking and they prefer to conduct transactions while on the go. They have extensive product knowledge and, by the time they dial in, they are already sold on their choice of hotel. Because they want functionality and speed when booking, a mobile version of a distribution channel needs to be designed that caters to the needs of this segment. Hotels that understand this emerging segment provide booking options through mobile-friendly versions of their websites.

Some hotels are also looking into using a hotel guest's mobile phone to page the guest or forward instant messages. Mobile phones may even be used for direct one-to-one marketing opportunities. Some mobile phones can already be used to pay for purchases at vending machines, parking meters, cab rides, and other points of sale. Lodging operators are looking to tap into this trend as well.

VingCard, a manufacturer of entry systems, has developed a mobile phone usage for access control using near field communication (NFC) technology. A text message is sent to a guest before arrival that includes the assigned room number and a code. The guest can proceed directly to the assigned room, where the mobile phone (turned on) that has the arrival message including the code must be held close to the door lock. The door lock will pick up and verify the code, then grant access. That completes the check-in of a pre-registered guest.

Market Targeting

The objective of market targeting is to focus marketing efforts on a group that has the potential to respond to a marketing appeal and that the hotel is best able to serve. The process of evaluating different market segments for targeting should consider a segment's size and growth potential, as well as its structural attractiveness. Structural attractiveness refers to such issues as age diversity, income brackets, geographic distribution, and whether it is easy to reach the segment through advertising channels. Analysis may show that, although the initial idea was not bad, a cluster of potential customers is too complicated to reach, too resource-intensive to locate, or not likely enough to respond to marketing efforts. A segment may look attractive, but the decision to select it for targeting must also consider the existing competition.

During the 1980s, companies were looking for the customer in each individual. That changed in the 1990s, when companies started to look for the individual in each customer. Today, a balanced approach that considers both the purchase intentions of customers and the customization capabilities of service providers concurrently seems to be more promising.

There will also be quantifiable issues to consider even when a proposed booking comes from the target market. For example, if accepting a group booking is consistent with a chosen market mix strategy (in terms of transient/group capacity allocation), but the chosen group needs rooms only and it is unwilling to book meals, this factor must be addressed in the decision to accept or reject the business.

There are other concerns as well. Assume a hotel has a group room block of 100 units to sell on a given day four months out. The forecast suggests that, at the group rate of $100, there is a probability that 80 percent will sell. That would generate $8,000 in room revenue and leave 20 units unsold from the room block. So far, there are only tentative bookings that need confirmation before the cutoff date, which is still one month away. What should a revenue manager decide if he receives a firm booking request for that date for 100 units at $60 per room? This offer would sell out the entire room block for a total of $6,000. Should he accept the firm offer of $60 because it is certain, or hold the rate at $100 in the hope that more lucrative bookings will arrive later as forecasted? The question is more important than the $2,000 revenue differential between the forecasted $8,000 and the firm booking for $6,000. This conundrum requires strategic thinking. The first question should be, What is the hotel's target market? Is it the $100 per room guests or is it the $60 clientele? If the revenue manager is comfortable that the hotel's product can be successfully marketed at the $100 price, there should be no reason to undermine that price positioning just to lock up an early booking.

Market Positioning

Once a hotel differentiates its value proposition, the next step is choosing a positioning strategy. A successful positioning strategy will be based on a set of possible competitive advantages that the hotel identifies. The chosen positioning needs to be communicated to target markets that are defined through segmentation. Generally, positioning strategies can be built on product attributes, price, or the needs a product or service can meet and the benefits consumers gain from buying it. There are also strategies to position against an existing competitor.

For example, a hotel may choose to position itself as a child-friendly property. A competitive advantage can be its proximity to an indoor water park that has wave pools, slides, and lazy river rides. The hotel may also develop special amenities such as a supervised kids activity center, enhanced safety and security, separate children's check-in station, games room, children's menu, and so forth. The needs for a safe and fun environment for kids are used for positioning. The benefit of a carefree vacation for parents is also emphasized.

Repositioning/Rebranding. One effective way to improve the revenue performance of underperforming hotels is repositioning. This effort frequently includes rebranding the property as well. The rebranding may include branding a non-branded hotel or switching brands. Some owners drop their brands and become independent through the repositioning, but that happens less frequently.

Repositioning a hotel down-market is often done when a hotel reaches a point in its life cycle when a major renovation becomes necessary to avoid functional obsolescence. Instead of a capital-intensive major overhaul, a hotel may choose a facelift only (new paint and furniture, but fixtures and building technology remain more or less the same) and a repositioning down-market. A struggling upscale hotel could become a competitive mid-tier one, or a mid-tier hotel becomes a budget hotel. New brand affiliation is usually part of the repositioning to facilitate financing and entry into a new market.

Repositioning up-market is also done on occasion, when opportunistic investors identify an underperforming asset that can be acquired at a reasonably low price in markets where unmet demand is identified for the high-end segment. Through renovation and major upgrades, a hotel can meet new criteria required to become a higher-category hotel. The process may involve installing a new management team and rebranding to acquire an affiliation consistent with the new market positioning. Astute investors are often able to unlock hidden potential through repositioning a hotel.

Promotion

Promotion is a next logical step in the strategic revenue management process. Promotion includes a blend of advertising, sales promotion, public relations, and personal selling. It can begin after differentiation and a market positioning strategy have been devised and a target market is identified. A hotel needs to communicate what it has to offer to its target market. The different ways of promoting the product help to create awareness and suggest action. Successful promotion leads to increased bookings.

A classic adage about advertising says, "Half the money I spend on advertising is wasted, but I don't know which half."[3] Targeted ads that deliver the right message to a carefully chosen segment using the most appropriate media mix can significantly improve the efficiency of advertising. The spending on television ads in recent years has declined, while the amount spent for online ads has increased. This trend is in response to the changing lifestyle and media consumption habits of the coveted higher-income, better-educated segment of consumers. With today's broadband infrastructure, mobile communication devices are used increasingly to deliver rich media content on top of voice and e-mail to subscribers using high-speed connectivity. *The Economist* projects the number of mobile phone users may reach four billion globally by 2011.[4] This trend opens promotional possibilities that many corporations are ready to exploit by shifting a growing proportion of their marketing budgets from offline to online media.

Customer Relationship Management

The theory and practice of *customer relationship management (CRM)* is a marketing field that has become more and more integrated with revenue maximization in recent years. The core concept of CRM is similar to the revenue management principle of identifying the highest-yield customers. It aims to generate more revenue through interacting with and retaining customers.

Any CRM system helps answer important questions of interest to a revenue manager:

- Who are my best customers?
- Why are they my best customers?
- How do I keep them?
- How do I find more like them?

The process starts with data analysis to help identify those guests that the hotel sees as having valuable revenue potential. By extracting information from the available data, revenue managers will be able to differentiate those groups who appear to be the best prospects for targeting. The next step is pattern detection and identifying how services and products could best be customized to cater to those patterns. At the execution stage, the value proposition has to be communicated to guests through the best-suited channels.

The growth in data volume and data sources has created a demand for better business intelligence using CRM. Many companies try hard to assemble a coherent picture of the customer from scattered information located throughout the entire enterprise. Marketers cull demographic and behavioral data from various sources, but it has been a challenge to gain accurate attitudinal data. Predictive analytics has successfully taken on that challenge and contributed to an improvement in CRM in this regard.

Predictive analytics, a relatively new tool, can not only determine a customer's propensity to buy, it can also forecast whether a customer will respond to a specific marketing appeal within a given time frame. Despite exponential growth in the quantity of data available, businesses can still achieve insight by making strategic decisions based on the quality of analysis. Predictive analytics is a growing field that has already led to a more dynamic customer experience by building on CRM and helping to maximize revenue potential at customer touch points.

Market Mix Management

Each hotel can tell for itself which of the market segments it serves is the most profitable. The objective of market mix management is to maximize profitability by allocating sufficient inventory to the most important segment(s). Market mix management is a strategic approach that may result in higher profitability at comparable or equal occupancy levels. Revenue growth is supported by selecting and booking the most profitable market group instead of less profitable groups vying for the same rooms. If a hotel allocates too much of its inventory to a less profitable segment, the revenue potential may not be fully maximized.

There is often significant temptation to accept bookings on first-come-first-served basis. But by allowing less profitable early bookings to take up most of the capacity, the shorter lead-time but much more profitable corporate segment could be squeezed out. It requires accurate forecasting and continuous monitoring of demand to find the right capacity allocation strategy for each week in order to optimize revenue generated from the mix of available customers.

The targeted market mix will be determined based on the individual hotel's capacity, location, classification, market position, bed configuration, and other factors such as affiliation, rating, age, etc.

Capacity. Smaller properties have to focus on a key segment of the market that they are best suited to target. Their market mix management can be a lot simpler than that of larger hotels. Midsize and large hotels are able to accommodate more travelers. These hotels need to develop room inventory allocation strategies. The larger a hotel, the stronger the need to get business from the group market and the meetings and conventions market. The ideal market mix of a 100-room hotel is different from the ideal market mix of a 1,600-room hotel.

These considerations are also subject to seasonality. A hotel may more aggressively pursue the group segment in shoulder seasons or off-seasons than in the main season, when it prefers higher-paying transient guests.

Location. A hotel's location has a lot to do with the mix of potential guests it appeals to. There are geographic regions with special features (such as climate, scenic beauty, historic sites, etc.) that influence both the seasonality and the nature of demand for accommodation. Business travelers favor locations considered major hubs of commerce. Some locations are known to be leisure getaway destinations, and some cities are major convention cities. Accessibility (e.g., direct flights), facilities, and climate are key factors. Destination marketing can also make a difference. Destination branding builds on reputations and image to develop branding for a given destination (e.g., the Big Easy; the Big Apple; What Happens in Vegas, Stays in Vegas; etc.). Hotels in urban markets will attract guests from different markets than suburban hotels, just as warm winter resorts have a slightly different customer mix than cold winter resorts. Prime location helps price positioning and provides more leverage in managing the mix of market demand.

Classification. Hotels can be classified by a number of factors. A hotel classified as a suburban midsize full-service branded hotel that targets the corporate traveler will probably have a market mix that consists of mostly individual transient business on weekdays. The same hotel may have a different market mix strategy to allocate more inventory to leisure groups on weekends and during the off-season, when the corporate market is soft.

Classification can determine the market orientation and price range of a hotel, leading to identifying primary and secondary (and even tertiary) market segments that will make up the market mix. Different classifications result in different market mix strategies.

Market Position. The market position of a hotel affects how dominant the hotel can become within its comp set. If a hotel controls a significant portion of the room inventory, it has more clout regarding rates and targeted market segments. A hotel that has no significant influence within its comp set is like a small fish in a big pond; it has to be keenly aware of market forces.

A dominant player in a comp set has more leverage to set trends and drive rates or introduce a segment into the market mix. If a hotel with a strong market position decides, for example, to pursue a health-conscious segment of the market through the addition of a spa, other hotels in the comp set will have to take note. Smaller hotels of the comp set may consider riding the same wave and introducing their own, less resource-intensive additions to cater to the needs of the new segment attracted to the market: alternative menus, upgraded gym equipment, and other wellness and fitness initiatives can be considered.

The market position of a hotel within its comp set will influence the decisions related to market mix strategy. There are leaders and followers.

Bed Configuration. The needs and wants of a market segment must be accommodated to earn the business of that segment. A hotel that decides to pursue family travelers has to be able to offer cribs, cots, extra beds, and adjoining rooms to cater to the needs of families traveling with any number of kids of all ages. If a hotel has only king-size beds, it will not appeal to travelers who want to share a room but not the bed.

Other. There are some other factors that may have a role in developing a market mix management strategy. A property's age is one. Older properties may have a better-established presence in a market. On the other hand, the physical shape of a property inevitably factors in the selection of a target market. Older buildings are a lot more challenging to keep up. Room size; amenities; building systems; and furniture, fixtures, and equipment are all tell-tale signs of aging. Although there are great examples of old landmark hotels being well capitalized and kept current through renovation and refurbishment, the more usual occurrence is that, as a hotel starts losing its luster, the change in the mix of the clientele follows more or less in sync with the physical deterioration of a property.

There is one more important consideration to keep in mind when developing a market mix strategy: some customer segments mix together better than others. One of the most critical intangibles any hotel can possess is called *ambience*. It is made up of a blend of smells, sounds, colors, objects, and the people that one experiences on the premises. Ambience can be carefully managed in order to provide guests with the feeling of being at a place where they are comfortable. Always keep in mind that other guests are part of the ambience. Therefore, a revenue manager should not allocate capacity to any segment that may potentially drive away members of a more important segment. The market mix on a given day must be balanced against strategic objectives.

For example, one resort hotel that had successfully built a good family-friendly reputation learned a lesson the hard way. One weekend, to fill a gap, the hotel booked a convention of "swingers" known for their adult lifestyle. The hotel received numerous complaints and bad media when concerned parents staying that weekend with kids objected to scantily clad members of the convention openly displaying lewd behavior. The market mix that day became a source of trouble. The important lesson for revenue managers is to be mindful of who will share elevator rides. Some market mix solutions result in a perfect blend, while others do not. The market mix strategy should consider which segments and clusters can be blended without negative repercussions.

Strategic Pricing

Pricing is both tactical and strategic. Pricing tactics are applied when dealing with short-term issues. Same-day and same-week pricing decisions are tactical in nature. The hotel's objective in those cases is to generate cash flow. If a hotel believes that a room rate adjustment will increase its sales revenue a given day or week, it will practice tactical rate management.

Strategic pricing has a different objective. It considers the long-term aspects of rate management to increase revenue by growing market share and improving market positioning. A hotel's strategy must be firmly grounded in market information and product quality. Inferior products will not earn a sustainable position in a competitive market. If a hotel has a poor product, no matter how well merchandised, it may not be able to build a loyal clientele of return guests over the years. Strategic positioning should align price point and product quality with target markets.

Competing on Price

The most important initial issue in strategic pricing is deciding whether a hotel will compete on price at all. The more a revenue manager knows, the less likely it is that he will recommend competing on price alone. The main problem is that any competitor can beat any low rate any time it wants to. The competitor may be desperate enough to do it or may simply want to create some buzz in the market. Most hotels have other ways to generate demand that are both more sustainable and financially more lucrative than trying to be the lowest-price operator in a market.

Some managers mistake the value perception of customers for price sensitivity. The customers' perception of value is created by a number of product attributes other than price.

Is price the most important driver of purchase decisions? Research that looked extensively at value drivers discovered that price was the third most important item for business travelers staying in economy and midrange hotels, behind property type/location and amenities. It was the main value driver for the same customer segment when booking upscale hotels. Price was second behind amenities for leisure guests selecting economy hotels, but the key factor for leisure guests when selecting upscale and midrange hotels.[5] Another interesting finding was the guests' willingness to pay up to 10 percent higher rates for enhanced safety and security. Another survey found that 38 percent of online bookers were willing to pay up to 20 percent higher room rates for customized services. These survey results indicate that low price alone is not necessarily the most important selection criterion for a significant portion of hotel guests.

If price is not always the most important decision driver at booking, then the strategic choice to make price the primary competitive weapon must be considered with extreme care. Competing on price may work well for some hotels in certain markets, but it is definitely not for all hotels in all markets.

The objective of matching competitors' price points is to be on par with the competition. In most jurisdictions, a hotel cannot directly discuss product pricing with its peers and competitors because that would violate antitrust laws and regulations designed to protect consumers from price gouging. But it is legal for revenue managers to monitor the competitors' rates. Based on the price changes in a given comp set, a hotel may decide to adjust its own rates. A hotel might make the strategic choice to stay close to the rate levels of comparable products. There are pros and cons to such a strategy.

The first problem is control: who is in charge of a given hotel's rate management? If a hotel feels compelled to blindly follow every price move up or down of its competitors, the question is a valid one. Another hotel may read the market dynamics better or it may interpret them poorly. Revenue managers should do their own thinking and strategy development, not just mirror others' actions. Another issue is the fact that the cash flow situation and the product costs of a competitor may be different, and those factors may provide their motivation for room rate changes. Revenue managers should know better than to change their own rates due to the operational challenges of competitors. If a hotel's revenue manager doesn't know why a hotel in the comp set is changing room rates and is not being pressured by operational issues, why would she be eager to meet price changes? Frequent price changes can also confuse customers.

On the positive side, the perception of the market needs to be considered. Guests shopping for accommodations at a destination may need to see comparable prices in order to encourage them to look further into other product attributes. In order to prevent a booking decision made on rates, take the rate difference out of the picture. Then let the location, service quality, brand power, or other differentiators become decision drivers. If preserving market share is a concern, a hotel may need to match discounted rates. If a competitor raises rates, these increases might be matched as well so the market will not perceive one hotel's product as inferior simply because it's cheaper.

A hotel may or may not choose to set competitive rates. Nonetheless, revenue managers should always monitor rates in their comp set and act on rate changes if there is a justifiable reason that is consistent with a chosen pricing strategy.

Pricing Strategy and Market Share. Research has shown that hotels that hold their rates and do not pursue a strategy of underpricing competitors achieve higher RevPARs. If a hotel's strategic objective is to do anything to increase market share, then strategically positioning its room rates lower than those of the comp set will provide results (at the cost of financial performance). The gain in market share is not likely to be solid, though. Guests who are price-loyal will always base their booking decisions on price and go wherever they get a lower rate. Should there be another hotel in the market one day with a steeper discount or a better deal, the price-driven clientele will probably switch without hesitation. This game of "price limbo" cannot be won with certainty.

Physical Rate Fences. Room rate management may use physical rate fences to differentiate similar value propositions. Examples include the size and location of a room, the view, bed configuration, and the presence or absence of amenities (hair dryer, robe, separate check-in counter, high-speed wireless connectivity, DVD player, iPod docking station, HD television, fruit plate, etc.).

Non-Physical Rate Fences. Non-physical rate fences can also have an impact on price points. Examples include the season of the year, time of booking (same-day or advanced booking), membership (loyalty program, associations), form of payment (non-refundable, full advance payment in exchange for a lower rate), booking channel (lower rates for hotel-direct Internet bookings), volume discounts (group rate), and so forth.

Rate Parity

Competitive pricing is based on keeping up with competitors. In contrast, *rate parity* is focused on a given hotel's own rate management practice. Rate parity means offering the same room rate for the same room night, regardless of distribution channel (e.g., voice or Internet) or booking mechanism (e.g., direct or third-party).

While hotels may strive for rate parity, it has often been difficult to achieve. When there is rate *dis*parity, bookers will find different rates for the same room night based on distribution channels. The chances are good that they will exploit the differences. If they can find a rate lower than the hotel-direct rate, they will take it.

As an unspoken acknowledgment of rate disparity, many hotels have initiated highly successful "best-rate guarantees" that promise to meet or beat the rates of third-party resellers. These guarantees have driven the majority of room bookings back to a business-to-customer model, thus taking the bulk of room bookings back from third parties. It is a key issue for hotels because there are cost differentials between bookings. Even when the same rate is offered to guests, the hotel's *net* rate may be different depending on the unit cost per booking associated with non-hotel-direct bookings. Revenue managers should remember to consider the net rate for decision-making purposes.

Customers prefer transparent pricing. If the same product can be had at different price points, customers may begin to wonder what it is they are actually paying for. Too many price points and complex pricing tend to lead to confusion (although customers will remain clear-headed enough to book the lowest price). The simpler a pricing strategy is, the more manageable it becomes both for hotels and their customers.

Revenue Streams Management

Most hotels have several revenue centers providing revenue streams. Different revenue streams typically have different contribution margins, so sales in one department can be more or less profitable than equal sales in another department. Even within a single department, different items can have different contribution margins. In the food department, for example, steak dinners usually have a higher margin than chicken dinners. Premium beverage brands have higher margins than the hotel's well brands. A failure to understand the importance of revenue stream margins can lead a manager to increase gross sales in a way that actually has a very small effect on net revenue.

As a simple example at the departmental level, consider a hotel that has $10 million in sales revenue derived from rooms, food, and beverage sales. In hotels having these three revenue centers, room sales almost always produce the highest contribution margin, followed by beverage sales, and then food sales. Assume this sample hotel has a revenue breakdown and contribution margins as follows:

	Gross Revenue	Percent of Gross Revenue	Contribution Margin	Net Revenue	Percent of Net Revenue
Rooms	$7,000,000	70%	85%	$5,950,000	74.4%
Food	2,000,000	20%	65%	1,300,000	16.2%
Beverage	1,000,000	10%	75%	750,000	9.4%
Total	$10,000,000			$8,000,000	

Note that room revenue is 70 percent of gross revenue, but that it accounts for more than 74 percent of the hotel's net revenue. The net revenue percentages for food and beverages are smaller than their gross revenue percentages.

Revenue streams management, also called *revenue mix management,* involves making decisions on the basis of contribution margin information. Revenue managers need to know what the margins are for the various revenue streams in order to know which streams to focus on for better financial results. The fundamental purpose of revenue streams management is to maximize profitability by focusing on the most profitable revenue streams and increasing their volume within the total. A conscious effort is made to increase revenue from the more profitable (higher margin) revenue streams. For example, it is more desirable to generate rooms revenue than function space revenue. When negotiating a group contract, a hotel should focus more on food and beverage revenue than on audiovisual equipment rental or meeting room decoration upgrades. Efforts spent on negotiating for (low margin) ice carvings should rather be spent on negotiating for premium beverage brands. Revenue streams management decisions may also affect the allocation of marketing and other resources.

Strategic Packaging

If a hotel is happy with its revenue performance, it has no pressing financial need to develop packages. However, if a hotel would like to generate more revenue through higher occupancy and/or higher per capita spending, it may consider strategically packaging a variety of products and services. A complex product can at times be more appealing to guests than offering rooms only. This strategy is somewhat underrated and underused because effective packaging takes work. When created and marketed well, however, packaging can increase both occupancy and overall revenue.

When a hotel offers products and services bundled with room nights, it is called a package. Although there are no rules about how many components a package should have, the traditional notion is that it will have at least two items in addition to the room accommodation. The addition of only one item (say, a breakfast) is not widely considered a package in marketing terms. A simple package with room, meal, and transportation is often an appealing one. The most frequently offered packages include food and beverage, transportation, entertainment, and/or wellness and fitness components.

A hotel may choose to apply discounted rates to a package, making the package cost less than the components would cost if purchased separately, *but it doesn't have to*. Discounting any or all components is at the discretion of the service providers. Hotels may believe that discounting will help sell the package, but they may also create packages that are so attractive they don't need to be discounted. Customers may perceive value even at full rates if a package is well composed, creative, and meets the needs and wants of carefully targeted customers.

In order to make the right decision regarding the delicate issue of pricing and discounting, a hotel needs to consider the price sensitivity of the targeted market segment, as well as how its package measures up to its competitors' packages. Is there a special element in the package? The more unique a package is, the better its chances to generate interest without discounting. The most challenging and resource-intensive aspects of package development are finding the concept, the theme, and the targeted market segment. Pricing comes well after that homework is done.

The Package Development Process

The package development process must always begin with a careful look at data. If package development is based on supposition instead of solid data, it becomes a gamble. Responsible managers prefer not to gamble. Data (independent facts) can be trusted. Data won't lie and it doesn't have an agenda.

What data should be considered? First we analyze what we already know about our own business need. A CRM system is a great source of information. A hotel will want to identify:

- The guests' reason for staying at a hotel (business, pleasure, or both).
- The average length of stay.
- The average dollar amount spent per guest (broken down to room and others).
- The average lead time and method or channel of booking.
- Rate and occupancy data by season to identify high, low, and shoulder season.
- High and low RevPAR days of the week.

This process of data interpretation can lead to a better understanding of a hotel's clientele. Is it necessary to dig deeper when mining data? If it makes business sense in order to fine-tune the market segmentation, a revenue manager may want to collect information (using observation, survey questionnaires, outside consulting firms, etc.) regarding the geographical market served. (Where do most of our guests come from? What is their preferred means of transportation?) Demographic information can also be meaningful. (What age brackets do they belong to? What income brackets? What is the gender breakdown?)

Weekday and weekend packages may target different segments and offer different package elements based on the data mined and analyzed. Smart packaging shouldn't be based on guesswork. Sound research may allow the hotel to create packages that work for guests the hotel knows. Some packages can be developed to increase revenue from a dominant market segment, and other packages can be designed to generate greater demand from a smaller segment that has latent potential (the latter being an example of supply-induced demand).

The perception of value is the most critical aspect of package design. Packaging just for the sake of packaging is unnecessary and mistaken. The targeted customers need to perceive the value of packages. Each bundle has a chance to become successful only if it appeals to its audience. Suppose a hotel offers the choice of special dietary meal selections (organic, vegetarian, low carb, etc.) and babysitting services to go with a show featuring a superstar. It may get the attention of a health-conscious market segment that travels with underage kids and appreciates world-class entertainment. In this case, a discounted price is not likely to be the element that creates a perception of value: it would be the combination of carefully chosen elements hitting the right buttons for its intended target segment. We may have a winning package even at full rates.

Packages with Internal Components. One way to bundle items is to use only components that the hotel itself produces and controls. For example, a hotel might offer a "Weekend Getaway" package that includes transportation from the airport to the hotel, a welcome cocktail, a Saturday room night in a junior suite, and a dinner for two. In this case, the hotel offers its own shuttle bus for the transportation, its own lobby bar for the drink, and its own restaurant for the meal. This way, the hotel has the highest level of control over the total package in terms of quality, price, and other product attributes (menu selection, room location, etc.).

Internal packages are easier to develop because they require less coordination, and they are less labor-intensive to develop because the developing department doesn't have to scout, rank, and qualify external service providers. The risk of anything going wrong or of being forced to troubleshoot is also significantly smaller. The hotel that offers only its own products in a bundle would know in time if a vehicle is being serviced at the shop, an employee called in sick, or a suite is out of order. Corrective measures can be taken and guests may not even notice if a minor change becomes necessary.

There is, however, a downside to internal bundles. A hotel has a finite number of items it can package, which will limit the possibilities if can offer. It is extremely difficult to offer a meaningful differentiation and generate excitement if a hotel lacks unique attributes. Sometimes the missing piece of the puzzle is not to be found inside one's hotel.

Packages with External Components. Given the limitations of packages containing only internal components, some hotels take on the challenges of teaming up with external service providers to create that spark that they hope will light up the switchboard. For example, a "Night on the Town" package might offer a room night, a drink, an event ticket, and a sightseeing tour. In this case, the hotel controls only the room and the drink. The event (a show or a sporting event) and the sightseeing tour are offered by outside operators. The hotel may negotiate favorable rates with a theater, convention center, arena, or major league sports franchise and a tour operator, but it has no control over those items.

A hotel may not have legal liability for a third-party mishap, but the hotel that is developing a package is responsible for screening and qualifying those businesses it partners with. A hotel that trusts its guests to another company's limousines, buses, eateries, or entertainment must know the product it offers in its bundle. Knowing does not come from phone conversations, websites, or hearsay. Testing, shopping, and experiencing the product is fundamental. We have to taste it, smell it, see it, and touch it in order to evaluate it and, if it is acceptable, to properly promote it to guests.

Some managers question the rationale of bundling external items with a hotel's room nights. They ask, "Why discount my rate to sell someone else's product?" There are various possible answers. A show or game ticket may help sell a room night that would otherwise remain unsold. In some packages, the external component may be the main demand driver. Just consider what a Super Bowl, a Grand Prix, or a Mardi Gras can do for a region's hotels. In these cases, hotels may benefit from the cross-marketing exposure and generate business as a result of their association with key external events, attractions, or shows.

The Objective of Packaging

Hotels in different markets use packaging for different purposes, but there is one common element. The fundamental purpose of packaging is to create *the perception of value*. If a hotel successfully creates an appealing value proposition at full rates that guests perceive as a good deal, discounts may be unnecessary. The temptation to discount can be significant, as dropping rates is a lot easier than going through the trouble of creative package development. But great packages can distinguish hotels and help them earn business.

A significant difference exists between the objectives of urban commercial properties and resort hotels. The author and Hoffer Lee, an MBA student of the University of Guelph, conducted research which showed that the primary purpose for packaging in urban hotels was to boost occupancy, while resort properties offered packages to boost revenue in the first place. If a hotel has to compete in a fragmented metropolitan market, every meaningful point of differentiation matters. Attractive packages may become demand drivers if everything else (location, quality of service, rate, amenities, loyalty programs) are comparable.

The resort business is different. Even in a fragmented resort market, the packages offered by a resort hotel may not become critical factors at the point of purchase. Guests will consider prices, service quality, brand familiarity, amenities, and proximity to attractions (or the airport) before the packages of a hotel.

Note that vacation packages offered by tour operators show different dynamics. In those cases, consumers are dealing with a value proposition of a third party, not a service provider. Tour operators also benefit from revenue management strategies and tactics, but their primary source of income is the margin they realize by marketing a variety of service providers' products. In a vacation package, the transportation and the hotel are the key components; location, price, and the convenience of the schedule are also key decision drivers. For example, a guest may prefer an all-inclusive one-week vacation package that offers a Saturday departure over a similar package with a midweek departure date. In this case, the package differences offered by the competing hotels didn't even come into play. Regardless of each package's other components, the traveler's decision may be based on the practicality of the departure date.

Our research identified another difference: resort hotels seem to favor a high variety of different packages, while urban properties favor a smaller selection of high-content packages instead. Once a resort hotel got selected for a vacation that is sold in weekly blocks (for the most part), the arrangement includes a given meal plan. After the guest booked the vacation, the best way to maximize revenue for the hotel is to offer appealing packages of activities to guests after arrival. Whether it is golf, sailing, scuba diving, salsa dancing, or helicopter-skiing depends on the location and type of resort. Some destinations are rich in sights; day trips can be offered to visit historic sites and museums and to experience native culture. Other destinations have spa packages or capitalize on their close proximity to cities with great shopping or cultural points of interest. A high variety of packages can be effectively marketed to a captive audience at resort hotels, as the average length of stay is longer than that of urban commercial hotel guests.

City center hotels have to consider the shorter duration of stay and make the most of their amenities. That explains the rationale of smaller selection: a hotel may sell only one package per stay at best. The high content is necessary to compete with the destination's sightseeing offerings and to include as many of the hotel's own services as possible to maximize revenue opportunities. A good blend of internal and external components can get the attention of guests if promoted at the time of booking and/or at arrivals. The higher the content of internal items in a package, the more profitable it can become for the hotel.

Packaging and Segmentation

The importance of market segmentation was discussed earlier. Different market segments have varying needs and wants. The packages that are attractive to leisure travelers differ from the packages that business travelers find attractive. If a hotel has a well-defined approach to segmentation, customized packaging can be most effective. A corporate traveler may not be enticed by free parking or a coupon to the local zoo. However, leisure guests driving their own cars and traveling with kids will welcome packages that include an entrance to a theme park, free valet parking, breakfast, and unlimited video games played in the convenience of the guestroom using interactive television.

A business traveler may be more interested in high-speed wireless Internet, unlimited long-distance calls, and access to a board room or hospitality suite bundled with no-charge pay-per-view movies. The point is that each hotel must determine for itself the needs and wants of its clientele. It must also know intimately what its competitors offer. This way, differentiation and demand drivers can be managed successfully.

A current segmentation challenge has emerged since the mid-1990s: the combo package. Many commercial hotels have noticed that a growing segment of corporate guests tends to blend a day or two of leisure time with a business trip. For the first two nights, the guest may attend a conference, but on the third day, she becomes a tourist. The same guest in the same room at the same rate exhibits different buying behavior on the third night. Some brands are successful with pre- and post-event packages, custom packages, or dynamic packages in which guests select from a number of options to build their own package. This may involve air, car rental, local attractions, entertainment, gambling, or spa visits.

Packaging and Revenue Streams Management

It is important for hotels to identify the profitability of each component in a given package. Food and beverage products have different margins than room nights, and guided sightseeing tours or car rental margins differ from spa treatments. High and low margin items may be bundled together, but the overall revenue impact and profitability implications need to be clearly identified and aligned with the hotel's strategic marketing purposes.

There is tremendous potential in value-added packaging. Guests prefer one-stop shopping. Convenience is the driver, and good packages offer that. Sometimes, guests design their own packages and cherry-pick what they need. The hotel that offers both the technology and well-trained guest service agents (or a concierge) to take care of all guest requests can generate more revenue than those hotels that can't or won't meet their guests' unique needs. If a guest need make only one call to arrange for a table in the hotel's restaurant, for a pickup of items that need dry cleaning, for a massage in the hotel's spa, and for a limousine, the hotel is much more likely to maximize its revenues.

Another guest preference that has been demonstrated since the 1990s is inclusiveness. The drivers in this case are both value and convenience. Guests don't like to be nickeled-and-dimed. They find it annoying to be charged separately for local calls, Internet access, a coffee and muffin breakfast, or using the fitness facilities. More and more guests expect more and more services to be included in the room rate. All-inclusive resorts and cruises have been gaining popularity steadily.

From the service providers' perspective, value-added packaging is a well-invested effort that helps generate more revenue, boost occupancy, and maximize profitability.

Distribution Channel Management

Revenue managers work with a variety of distribution channels concurrently. The strategic objective of distribution channel management is three-fold. Managers try to obtain most of the hotel's revenue through those channels that are (1) the highest revenue producers, (2) the most cost-effective, and (3) the most easily controlled. The challenge to balance these criteria should not be underestimated.

It is important to identify which distribution methods and channels are able to reach a hotel's target market. The cost per booking also must be factored in when the net revenue is affected by the distribution channel.

Hotels can obtain reservations directly or indirectly. Both methods use a variety of distribution channels. In the direct-to-guest approach, a hotel can accept bookings directly from the guest in person; on the hotel's website; on the telephone; and in written communication using e-mail or text messaging, faxes (which are being used less and less frequently), and mail (which is fast becoming obsolete). Many earlier methods of direct-to-guest reservations used as recently as the 1970s are already obsolete. The days of the telex or tele-writer, which combined an electric typewriter and a phone-line to establish real-time connection in order to produce a written record, are long gone. It is a safe prediction that, in the not too distant future, the fax machine will follow the fate of the telex. Written communication is becoming increasingly keyboard- or keypad-based.

When there is an intermediary between a guest and a hotel in the process of booking, the method becomes indirect. The most common intermediaries are travel agents, tour operators, demand collectors (web portals), central reservation services (CRSs), destination management services (DMSs), global distribution systems (GDSs), and call centers of representation agencies, referral services, and marketing alliances. Each intermediary can drive revenue to a given hotel. Revenue managers need to maintain good working relationships with all of them. The source analysis of revenues will identify which partners are main revenue producers. The ratio of revenue production per intermediary might vary depending on the season of the year, the target market, or other circumstances. There are hotels that get most of their off-season revenue from travel agents, but directly book their own transient guests in the main season.

All the above methods of booking use either voice, the GDS, or the Internet for communication and actual transaction purposes. The methods of distribution and the channels available can be combined in any way.

Voice Channels

Hotels can use direct lines connected to their reservation office, front office, or PBX to take bookings. The number of hotel guests who are comfortable booking their stay without intermediaries is growing, but the growth is not on the voice channels. Call volume on voice channels has been decreasing since the turn of the century. At the same time, the conversion rate is up, meaning that a higher percentage of calls end up with closing a sale. That can be attributed to better training of the reservation agents and the efficient use of guest history files that can speed up the booking process. Another contributing factor is the fact that a growing percentage of potential guests conduct their search for accommodation online before they place a call. While many customers are comfortable using the Internet to search for destination information, look up accommodation options, comparison shop, and even sift through guest reviews to see what past guests have to say about a specific operation, some still prefer to make the actual reservation by speaking with the chosen service provider.

There are various reasons for this phenomenon. One is the doubt some guests have in the security of online payment methods, which leads them to switch to the telephone to complete their transactions. Another is the need to talk to a live agent who can answer relevant questions on product information and local particularities not found on the Internet. The point for revenue managers is to pay attention to customer preferences.

Operators serving the upscale market have learned the importance of personal interaction for their high-touch clientele. They may hesitate even to introduce automated voice systems that could replace reservation agents. Individual attention can be extremely important from the outset. An old adage says, "You never have a second chance to make a good first impression." For hotels, the first impression may happen long before the guest arrives, when the first call is placed to book the reservation.

Call centers of hotel chains or referral services offer an effective solution for handling high call volumes. However, the cost per booking may increase and the service quality may be lower. Reservation agents employed at the property level may have better product knowledge and more motivation to upsell. The importance of inside information should not be underestimated. Knowing about the renovation date of the pool, the channel selection of the cable package in guestrooms, a new chef being hired, and the trendy new curved shower curtain rods can help close a sale.

Revenue maximization strategies will have to include voice channels for the foreseeable future.

GDS Channel

The global distribution system was "the" electronic channel before the Internet emerged. The GDS offers an important channel that hotel revenue managers use to connect with travel agencies and other demand collectors. It started out as the central reservation system for the airline industry in the late 1970s. It was made necessary because travel volume had increased to such a level that manual systems became too slow and labor-intensive. It was made possible by new electronic data processing that emerged as a result of the evolution in microprocessors. The GDS was designed to facilitate airline bookings in the first place. Travel agents found that booking through the GDS was cost effective. Hotel and car rental bookings became an add-on in the 1980s.

Some operators of high-end hotel chains were reluctant to offer online booking engines on their websites in the late 1990s, at a time when most other hotel chains had started doing so. Their reasoning was that most of their clients were already online with them through the GDSs and that senior executives, wealthy individuals, and the group guests who made their critical volume were not expected to start booking their stays themselves. They still entrusted their office or travel agent to book their trips, and those bookings were done online already through the GDS. Times have changed. It is unusual today to find a hotel website without booking capability.

The major players are SABRE, Apollo, WorldSpan, and Amadeus. The reservations processed through their networks have to go through switching companies to interface with the service providers. Although the GDS has traditionally been a business-to-business (B2B) model, the evolution of electronic travel transactions facilitated by the Internet has offered new opportunities to GDS businesses that were too good to pass up. A number of GDS companies extended their business by launching consumer websites and offering hotel inventory to online agencies as well. The traditional role of managing the traffic between suppliers and distributors has evolved to something more complex. The volume booked through the GDS will keep it relevant to revenue managers for years to come.

Internet Channels

The Internet has changed the way business is conducted. It took a number of years for the hotel industry to unlock the potential of the Internet, and the learning curve was steep. In the late 1990s, when businesses started to establish their presences online, it was mostly considered a promotional opportunity with little direct revenue impact. However, as the household penetration of the Internet started to grow exponentially, the software applications to get online became a lot more user-friendly. As a consequence, more and more businesses seized the chance to realize first-mover advantage in the new field of e-commerce.

The early years of the "tech bubble" were exciting and turbulent times, when the emergence of Internet-based businesses resulted in a lot of start-ups. After the dust settled, it became evident that choosing the Internet as a platform would add the most value to those businesses that could not do what they were doing without the Internet. Some of those online businesses allowed customers to search travel information, book a travel service or product quickly and easily, process payment, and issue confirmation around the clock, and these sites became very popular.

Around the turn of the century, the hotel industry allowed third parties to collect demand and act as intermediaries between hotels and guests. Hotels initially considered online resellers to be a convenient additional distribution channel generating new revenue: the agencies did all the work of investing in the technology; building the online businesses, web portals, and booking engines; and finding the customer and selling the product to them. It took a few years before the industry realized the magnitude of revenue leakage (measured in billions of dollars) that this approach allowed. The industry finally responded, and the B2C direct distribution model emerged as the most important Internet distribution model as a result.

B2C Model (Hotel Direct). When guests book their stay with a hotel or hotel brand without an intermediary, it is called a *B2C (business-to-customer) model.* This Internet-based direct distribution model is the most profitable because it is the most cost-effective, and hotels have the highest level of control over this model of distribution.

The hotel industry started to get seriously interested in taking back control over their product distribution when after 2000, a record year for the tourism industry, demand started to dwindle. The events of September 11, 2001, accelerated and worsened the decline in travel and tourism, and the hotel industry went through cost cutbacks and deep discounting. It became obvious that revenue generation was the only way forward, and the interest in revenue management strategies and tactics grew. The analytical approach highlighted the importance of profits taken by online resellers (revenue leakage). This became a point of contention by 2003, when hoteliers realized that instead of tapping into new revenue sources, the online booking intermediaries were tapping into existing customers who simply had new buying behaviors.

The strategic response needed was evident: hotels had to try to take back control and sell most of their capacity themselves, directly to the customers, bypassing intermediaries. The keys to success were in understanding the online distribution channels and their dynamics. This understanding was then coupled with improvements both in the technology (transaction speed, real-time dynamic pricing, availability controls, search engine optimization, etc.) and the appearance and design of the hotels' websites (web portals). Sites were redesigned to offer faster downloads and clarity to help users find what they wanted within a couple of clicks. The sites began to offer booking capability and relevant links (to maps, local weather, events, attractions, etc.) on the landing page.

On top of user-friendly websites and cutting-edge technology, the direct distribution model needed to make it worthwhile for the guest. Best-rate guaranties were offered and guests voted with their mouse clicks. Direct bookings through the Internet started to grow significantly. By the second half of the decade, the hotel industry successfully took back control over the sales of the majority of room nights sold over the Internet. The direct B2C model has proved to be the best contributor to hotel revenue growth and profitability.

Harnessing the Internet and exploiting its opportunities are absolutely critical in today's business environment. The most popular online activity after checking and sending e-mails is the use of a search engine. Leading online behavioral research groups reported in 2007 that as much as 70 percent of all Internet activity began with a search engine. This was consistent for men and women and across demographics and socioeconomic levels. Sixty-four percent of online users start with a search engine for travel-related searches.

Search engines want to see content when they visit a website. Content-rich pages appeal to both website visitors and to search engine spiders, and creating such pages can help a hotel achieve higher visibility. The use of relevant keywords can drive both online and offline sales. The number of keywords used per page and the frequency of website updates containing fresh content affect search engine visibility.

SEO (search engine optimization) also looks at link popularity, building on one of the most important algorithms that the major search engines use: determining who is linking to a given website. Websites can rank higher on search engines based on the quality and relevancy of links pointing back to the website.

Hotel brands that are successful in their efforts to stay relevant and connected to their customers go beyond search engine marketing and embrace the social Internet or Web 2.0 and new media formats such as consumer-generated media (CGM)—exemplified by Facebook, YouTube, and Trip Advisor—blogs, wikis, and other fast-evolving forums and channels. Mobile Internet usage patterns also show a significant growth in data access.

Agency Model. The *agency model* is based on simple straight commissions. There is no commitment for any of the parties in terms of capacity allotment or rate, and if an Internet travel agency can find a guest for a room night, based on availability, the hotel pays a commission, often around 10 percent of the room rate, in recognition of the business. This model gives the hotel a high level of control over price and availability. However, the volume driven through this Internet distribution model is not significant compared with the other models.

Merchant Model. For online merchants, the *merchant model* became the most successful Internet business model for selling hotel capacity and related products. Internet-based businesses serving the travelers' every need became highly successful investments as the traveling public began to use the Internet. According to penetration statistics, the online travel market as a percentage of the total travel market grew from 42 percent in 2005 to 60 percent in 2008 in the United States, and from 15 to 41 percent in Europe.

The concept of the merchant model is not new to the hotel industry. Hotels have used a similar deal structure for many years when dealing with wholesalers. This model is based on an agreement between the hotel and the e-merchant that allows the online agency to take a hotel's negotiated capacity allotment with a cut-off date at BAR (best available rate) and mark it up to resell it to customers. The usual mark-ups are in the 20–30 percent range and the sell rate is controlled by the online agency. The most successful examples are expedia.com, travelocity.com, and hotels.com.

Revenue managers cannot afford to ignore online agencies, regardless of the business model they follow. However, it was important for the industry to learn that in the period between 2000 and 2004, the merchant model eroded price parity. Hotels gave up control over the prices of their rooms and in some cases ended up competing with themselves when an online agency decided to undercut the hotel's rates for last-minute customers. It is also important to point out that the listing of hotels on a merchant's website follows one significant criterion: hotels are ranked by their production for the merchant. That is an astute approach by the merchant, as it provides an incentive for business partners to be high producers and appear on the top of a list, because half of customers on average choose from the first screen; they do not proceed to the second screen of a lengthy listing of available hotels. Half of the viewers who go to the second page do not look at a third.

The ranking of a hotel in a search result clearly can significantly affect the probability of getting a booking. Online merchants have an interest in promoting those hotels that are proven sources of revenue for them. When working with online merchants, hotel revenue managers need to see the facts and base their strategy on a lucid understanding of the business model.

Hybrid Model. The *hybrid model* is a combination of the merchant and agency models. Online agencies may choose to offer a package of products with somewhat lower mark-ups and certain strings attached for consumers: non-refundable payment on booking; minimum three-day advance purchase, after which no changes are allowed; etc. A frequently offered bundle includes air transportation, a room selection from among participating hotels, and a car rental.

The sales tactics of online agencies include bundled and unbundled (hotel-only) product offerings. If that's the case, the ranking offers the merchant model items first, followed by agency model constructs.

Opaque Model. The *opaque model,* also called a *reverse auction,* has been quite successful on the customer side with brand-neutral hotel guests who book at the last moment. An opaque site (priceline.com and hotwire.com are the best known) lets the customer describe his or her needs and name a price that he or she is willing to pay. If a hotel meets the criteria (location, service level, and price), the customer must prepay before learning which hotel he or she just booked with. Because of the initial anonymity, hotels can dump distressed inventory on opaque sites to pick up incremental business without damaging their rate integrity.

The opaque model is a good example of a business solution that could not exist without the Internet. Under this model, the hotel offers rooms to the site at a net rate that the customer will not see. The opaque site matches customers to hotels that meet their criteria. The opaque site will take the payment from the customer and will keep the difference between the hotel's net rate and the rate offered by the customer.

Endnotes

1. Linda Canina and Steven Carvell, "Lodging Demand for Urban Hotels in Major Metropolitan Markets," *CHR Reports* 3, no. 3 (2003). Available at www.hotelschool.cornell.edu/research/chr/pubs/reports/abstract-13608.html.
2. *Tourism Daily,* April 26, 2007.
3. John Wanamaker (1838–1922), U.S. department store magnate.
4. *Economist,* April 28, 2007.
5. R. Verma, G. Plaschka, C. Dev, and A. Verma, "What Today's Travelers Want When They Select a Hotel," *HSMAI Marketing Review* (Fall 2002).

References

Bender, D. (2007). "12 Technologies and Trends that Are Transforming Digital Marketing." *HSMAI Marketing Review.* Winter 2006–07.

Burns, J., and J. Inge. (2004). "Hold Your Horses! Getting a Grip on the Reins of Distribution Channel Management." *Hospitality Upgrade.* Summer.

Canina, L., and C. A. Enz. (2006). "Revenue Management in U.S. Hotels: 2001-2005." *CHR Reports* 6, no. 8.

Coy, J., and B. Haralson. (2005). *Hotel Waterpark Resort Industry Report 2005.*

Enz, C. A., and L. Canina. (2005). "An Analysis of Revenue Management in Relations to Hotels' Pricing Strategies." *CHR Reports* 5, no. 6.

Enz, C. A., and G. Withiam. (2003). "Evolution in Electronic Distribution: Effect on Hotels and Intermediaries." *CHR Reports* 3, no. 5.

Green, C. E. (2004). "De-Mystifying Distribution: Building a Distribution Strategy One Channel at a Time." *HSMAI Marketing Review.* Fall.

Haley, M., and J. Inge. (2005). "Revenue Management: It Really Should Be Called Profit Management." *Hospitality Upgrade.* Fall.

Chapter 5 Outline

Competencies

1. Describe automated revenue management systems, including their capabilities and the cultural and system-integration challenges they present to hotels. (pp. 95–99)
2. Explain how the revenue manager position evolved, and identify typical tasks and competencies of revenue managers. (pp. 99–104)

5

Revenue Management's Place in Hotels

REVENUE MANAGEMENT SYSTEMS and the revenue manager position itself have grown in complexity and sophistication in the past two decades. In this chapter, we will first look at the capabilities of automated revenue management systems and the challenges associated with implementing these systems in hotels, then conclude the chapter with a discussion of how the position of revenue manager was created and has evolved within hotel companies.

Revenue Management: Automated Systems

Why are revenue management systems in hotels so complex? The simple answer is that the systems are complex because the revenue management task is complex. Revenue management encompasses controlling the availability of inventory units involving multi-tiered pricing structures; selling different room types; deploying various capacity-management tactics; and controlling and monitoring other revenue management components, many of which are subject to constant changes. Hotel decision-makers must process a lot of data.

Accuracy and immediacy are critical expectations of hotel managers. In today's world, revenue reports and other data outputs must be bulletproof and available at any time, through any point of access, whenever needed. The natural response to all of these needs, once computers came onto the scene, was to automate. Computers can perform complex computations at amazing speeds, and software programming has now reached a level where algorithm-based programs can deal with almost any possible set of variables in any scenario a manager can conceive, be it for a single hotel or a multiple-property company.

There are two basic types of automated revenue management systems—recommendation systems and decision systems:

- *Recommendation systems* are capable of monitoring, forecasting, and making recommendations for optimum revenue management solutions. Systems of this kind need actively involved revenue managers and analysts to input data, analyze system outputs, and make and implement sound decisions.
- *Decision systems* go one step further. Beyond the monitoring and forecasting functions, decision systems arrive at solutions that they consider optimum, then put in place all of the rate and capacity allocation controls necessary to achieve targeted results. Systems of this kind need revenue analysts for

data input and monitoring, plus revenue managers to supervise and override system-implemented controls if necessary.

Capabilities of Automated Systems

Both recommendation systems and decision systems are capable of performing vital revenue management tasks that are labor-intensive and tedious (as well as error prone) if done manually, such as:

- Forecasting demand
- Forecasting availability
- Analyzing data (key metrics of measurement)
- Quoting rates
- Optimizing (rate, occupancy, channels, segments, revenue streams)
- Analyzing comp sets
- Analyzing group business (and perhaps performing displacement analyses)
- Providing user-defined consolidated reports

Some revenue management system suppliers include budgeting capabilities in their systems as well.

Some system vendors promise a quantifiable improvement in revenue, either in the form of a 4 to 12 percent RevPAR increase or a 6 to 12 percent revenue lift, as a result of installing their system. The accuracy of such highly ambitious claims is subject to question, however.

Some revenue management systems need hardware as well as software installations. Vendors offer client-server solutions for a single property or small groups of properties. A pay-as-you-go ASP (Application Service Provider) solution is also available for interested clients. Training and consultation are customary components of product offerings. The market has become very competitive, and today revenue management automation solutions can be purchased for properties of all sizes and types.

Single-Image Inventory. The concept of single-image inventory is an important advance in revenue management automated systems that deserves special mention. Before this feature became available, hotels allocated blocks of their room inventory to in-house units (their front office, reservations office, and hotel sales office) and resellers (e.g., call centers, central reservations offices, global distribution systems, and travel agencies), and updated the reservations for the given blocks on a regular basis one or more times a day.

As a result of different blocks of rooms being controlled by different sellers, it was not unusual to experience inaccuracies, double bookings, or other forms of confusion from the operator's perspective. From the perspective of guests, different sellers meant they sometimes had to work harder to book a room. After being denied availability for a future date by the front office of a given hotel, for example, some consumers discovered that if they placed a call to the hotel's central reservations office, they might still be able to book a room, provided that the CRO's room block was not yet sold out at the time of the call. Of course, some consumers did not make the extra effort, and the hotel lost sales.

Single-image inventory means that interface technology has improved so much that availability information regarding each inventory unit, including designated room blocks, can be accessed in real time by all room sellers.

Consumers today can book a room night through a variety of distribution channels: by calling the reservations office of a hotel, accessing the website of the same hotel, calling the chain's central reservations office (if the hotel is part of a chain), or accessing the website of a third-party reseller. With single-image inventory, the product availability, rate rules, and all other relevant pieces of information are drawn from the same data source, so they are identical all the time, regardless of the point of access or the channel used. Any time a room status or price point is altered (a room night is booked or canceled, a discount implemented), the whole database that holds the information regarding each room's status for each night for years ahead must be updated instantly. The risk of double booking or losing a sale for the lack of up-to-the-minute information is practically eliminated by the capability of moving significant volumes of data very fast across cyberspace. Single-image inventory technology means that hotels' reservations information is accurate up to the second. When product availability information across all distribution channels becomes identical, single-image inventory (and rate parity) has been achieved.

The prevalence of this technology has helped eliminate duplication and confusion and has enabled hotels to capture maximum reservation volume while optimizing revenue.

Cultural Challenges of Automation

Both decision and recommendation revenue management systems require input from a hotel's revenue management team. The more appropriate and accurate the data that is input, the better the system's output. It happens frequently that a system forecast for occupancy for a future date provides a figure that experienced managers have a hard time accepting, and they may decide to override the system. What is remarkable is the proven fact that, in most such cases, the system's data has a tendency to be more accurate.

Overriding a system recommendation (e.g., a rate or minimum-stay requirement) is tempting for managers, and often there are good reasons to do so. Even if the system's recommendation for a two-night-minimum-stay restriction makes perfect sense under given market conditions, managers have to consider more than just tactical measures when dealing with guests. Even when demand is strong for multi-night reservations, the patronage of a high lifetime value guest who needs only one night is worth a lot more than the patronage of a first-time guest willing to make a two-night-stay booking but who may never return in the future.

High-end hotels have traditionally been hesitant to automate their revenue management operations, because they offer personal attention and intuitive and individualized services. Luxury hotel operators were concerned that if system outputs needed overrides too frequently, they would be more trouble than they were worth. Automation is a significant cultural change for such operations.

It is also not unusual to see managers who initially have a "Nintendo approach" to their new revenue management systems; that is, they play around with all the features and controls of the system and tweak settings too frequently, using a trial-and-error approach to learning about and implementing their systems.

Revenue management systems need to be given a fair chance to produce results, and patience is a very important virtue after implementation. Managers and employees have to learn gradually to appreciate what an automated system can do for them, and customize system settings only if there are strong reasons to do so. Revenue management systems are significant investments that can produce lucrative returns over time if used properly.

Having said that, it is also important to stress that the management of any business is best done by human beings. Artificial intelligence can contribute a lot to the decision-making process, but good managers never let a system take over. An optimum balance between automation and human intelligence can be achieved if managers let the systems do what systems do best, yet never let the human element take a back seat in an industry that takes pride in providing service to its customers.

System-Integration Challenges

In today's world even the smallest hotels have automated systems to help their managers with management tasks. Property management systems (PMSs); point-of-sale systems (POSs); accounting systems; customer relations management systems (CRMs); heating, ventilation, and air conditioning (HVAC) systems; and building transportation systems are examples of the different automated systems a hotel may use. Typically, hotels acquire different systems at different times from different vendors. It is a challenge for hotels to interface their different systems so that they work together and allow for seamless data transfer.

For example, think of the integration needed when a guest arrives back at the hotel after a business dinner with a client, swipes his room card to gain entrance to the parking garage, parks his car on the second underground level and then swipes his card again to enter the building from the garage, then swipes his card to use the elevator to access his floor. He swipes one more time to enter his room, where he takes a beer from the sensor-equipped mini bar as he sits down and turns on his laptop to check e-mail messages. Many automated systems were involved in this example: an access control system to enter the garage, the guest floor, and the room; the building transportation system to direct the elevator; the POS system and PMS system to post the charge of one beer (POS) to the room folio (PMS) and the charge for Internet usage if that is not free; plus a CRM system to pull all the guest's relevant data together to build a guest profile. These systems may have been acquired at different times from different vendors, but they still need to be interfaced. As you can see, there are challenges ahead when a vendor must install a revenue management system that will have to be interfaced with all of the existing systems of the hotel that service revenue centers.

When many properties at various locations need to be linked together, data has to be transmitted and shared among properties. To continue with our example, suppose the same guest is on the road again three months later. He books a room in a city he has never visited before, in a hotel of the same chain. If that hotel is provided with access to all of the information related to the guest's previous stay in the first chain hotel, a number of benefits occur: the booking process can be simplified and sped up, as the guest's personal information does not need to be collected again, only confirmed. His personal preferences regarding bed configuration, room location, and so forth can be automatically passed on to the second hotel. As a result of the streamlined reservation process, time is saved for both guest and hotel, and loyalty can be increased as a result of the wow factor—the hotel can certainly prove that this guest's business is appreciated and his needs and wants have been noted chain-wide.

In order to achieve this level of integration, a hotel chain has to go beyond property-level system integration and take integration to a regional, national, or even global level. It is hard enough to have all of the systems and sub-systems smoothly integrated at a single property; it is a significantly greater challenge to have all of a chain's different properties share data. The challenges of system integration are exponentially greater if the properties are in different time zones with different technological infrastructures and are staffed by people speaking different languages.

One interesting implication of data sharing concerns deciding who owns the data. Data ownership can become a highly significant issue if a franchise operation (one corporation) owned by another corporation, managed by yet another corporation, becomes the subject of a sales transaction. Is the data with all of its precious guest information the property of the franchisor company that installed and maintained the CRS, the management company that runs the hotel and serves the guest, or the owner/franchisee of the hotel? To prevent unnecessary confusion, in an ideal world this question is dealt with contractually at the outset.

Automation can be a key component in revenue management activities. However, the experience, sensibility, and intelligence of qualified managers and the service culture they create are the true sources of success. The human component can be complemented but never replaced or bypassed with automated systems in an industry that prides itself on customer service.

The Revenue Manager

When the new position of revenue manager was created, the position's responsibilities, task lists, and list of desired candidate qualifications had to be created as well. This all evolved gradually over time as the position matured. In the beginning, candidates for the new position were drawn from among those at the hotel who already had to deal with revenue-related issues. The traditional position of reservations manager at midsize and large properties with a reservations office was a logical place to start looking for candidates. Reservations as a process requires working with dates, availability information, rates, upselling, guest history files, and a number of other issues related to maximizing revenue. Therefore, it was quite common to find former reservations managers filling the first revenue manager posts with a reassigned position and a reclassified title.

Exhibit 1 Revenue Manager: Initial Stage

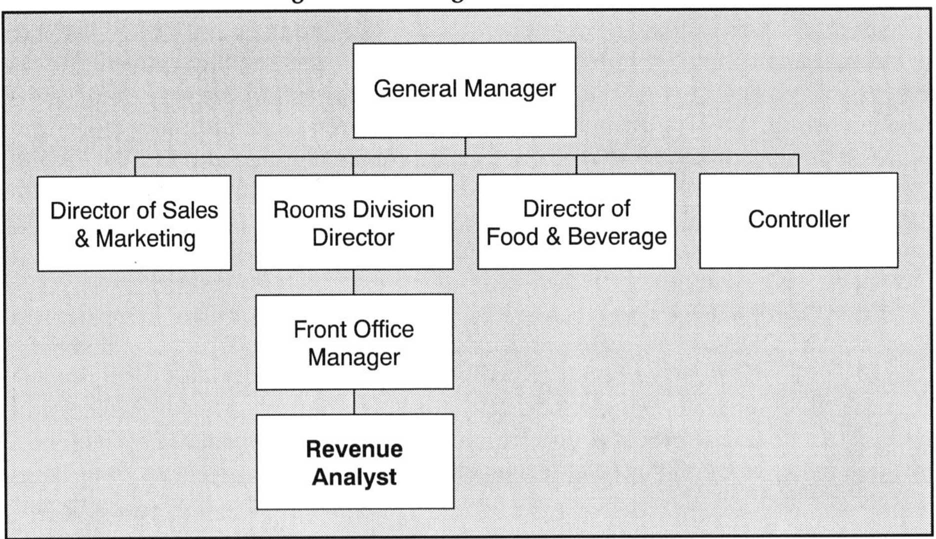

Over the years, the revenue manager position evolved as the new position's responsibilities and reporting relationships were fleshed out. The following sections discuss the stages of development of the revenue manager position.

Initial Stage. In the early days of revenue management, the newly minted revenue manager—often referred to as a revenue analyst—typically worked with the front office manager and most frequently reported directly to that position (see Exhibit 1).

At this initial stage, the reporting structure shown in Exhibit 1 was considered acceptable for a number of reasons. Only tactical-level involvement was expected from the revenue analyst/manager at this time, and only within the hotel's rooms division. The new revenue analyst/manager was involved in historic data analysis, forecasting, processing reservations, and producing reports with a focus on internal measurement metrics. The new position was expected to perform analytical tasks and provide input to the hotel's management staff, but no significant decision-making authority was delegated to this new position at this stage.

Intermediate Stage. After the new position of revenue analyst proved to be useful, over time it started to get recognized by other hotel managers for its significant role in tactical decision-making, and a re-alignment occurred within the rooms division (see Exhibit 2). This was the result of the growing emphasis in hotels on revenue maximization as a source of profitability.

In this intermediate stage, the revenue manager position indeed evolved into a management-level position on par with other hotel department heads, such as the front office manager. In this stage, the revenue manager may or may not have had a revenue analyst reporting to him or her, based on the size of the property and the responsibilities assigned to the manager. At this stage, the job still

Exhibit 2 Revenue Manager: Intermediate Stage

General Manager
- Director of Sales & Marketing
- Rooms Division Director
  - **Revenue Manager**
  - Front Office Manager
- Director of Food & Beverage
- Controller

involved mostly tactical-level activities, but it was more independent than in the initial stage, and there was a significant growth in authority. Giving the position a management title and management-level remuneration was a sign that upper-level hotel management recognized the complex nature of the job and the qualifications and experience required.

At this point, some key hospitality organizations (such as AH&LA and HSMAI) introduced specialized training and certification programs for revenue managers to complement the corporate programs and on-the-job training. A body of revenue management literature started slowly getting into industry magazines, and most lodging industry conferences and trade shows began including panel discussions, workshops, or presentations on revenue management. Special interest groups devoted to revenue management started to get established within some industry associations. It is fair to say that this intermediate stage reflects where the revenue management position was for much of the first decade of the twenty-first century.

Evolutionary Stage. The next stage of the revenue management position can be classified as evolutionary in the sense that the revenue manager is no longer within the rooms division (see Exhibit 3). This evolution is the result of the revenue manager's involvement in more than rooms revenue management. Other revenue streams—food and beverage, function space, gambling, etc.—are now also monitored, measured, manipulated, and controlled by the revenue manager. At this stage, the revenue management position is also considered a contributor to the hotel's strategic planning.

The revenue manager's involvement in higher-level strategic thinking comes as a result of the new discipline of revenue management having "grown up" to become a significant contributor to more than just short-term tactical aspects of hotel operation. In recent years, revenue management has become recognized as a core competency for conducting business in the field of hospitality and tourism.

Exhibit 3 Revenue Manager: Evolutionary Stage

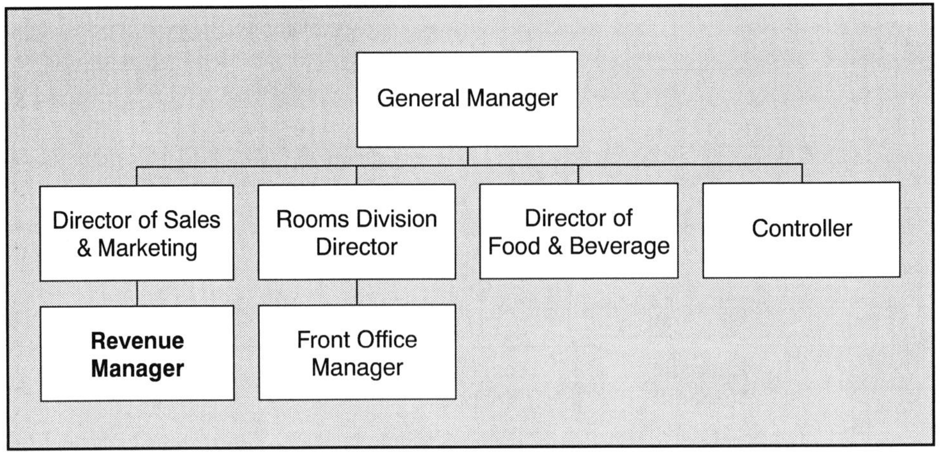

Exhibit 4 Revenue Manager: Fully Developed Stage

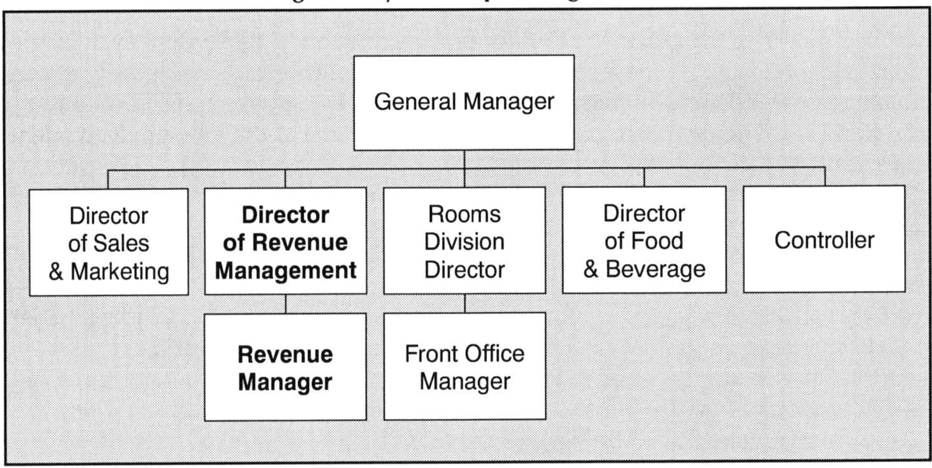

Today, many major international hotel corporations have revenue management expertise involved in all key management decisions. In fact, some of these companies skipped the evolutionary stage of revenue management and have already moved on to the next stage.

Fully Developed Stage. The significance of the changes to the revenue management position in the fully developed stage (see Exhibit 4) is evident: the revenue management function has been elevated to an executive-level position on equal standing with the other major functions of the hotel organization. The director of revenue management reports directly to the highest position in charge of operations, the hotel's general manager. This new organizational structure will eventually be embraced by all hotels that understand the vital role of revenue management, both on the strategic level with the inclusion of the director of revenue management position, and on the tactical level with the designation of a revenue manager on the same level as managers of other hotel departments.

The position of director of revenue management is involved in overarching strategic issues, with an emphasis on demand generation, market positioning, strategic pricing, market targeting, and promotion/advertising. The revenue manager should be involved in all of the other strategic aspects—e.g., distribution methods and channels, strategic packaging, etc.—plus all of the tactical aspects—e.g., forecasting, tactical rate control, stay control, and capacity management, among others.

Task Lists and Competencies for Revenue Managers

Probably the greatest pressure on revenue management professionals is the ever-increasing complexity and variety of tasks and competencies they are expected to master in order to optimize revenue.

Just as there are differences among hotels (midsize select-service properties versus large full-service properties, for example), there are differences among the task lists and responsibilities of revenue management professionals working in the hotels. Still, some commonalities can be identified. Forecasting, rate management, the analysis and evaluation of revenue management activities, report preparation, coordination with a variety of operational units, strategy development, and interaction with other managers are on the task list of every revenue management professional.

Core technical competencies required of revenue managers include the following:

- Managing group blocks
- Managing and monitoring Internet systems to ensure rate integrity and parity
- Managing the hotel's web portal
- Maintaining relationships with third party market managers
- Analyzing financial statements and market data
- Preparing accurate occupancy and revenue forecasts
- Developing tactics and strategies to manage group and transient market needs

The interpersonal competencies a revenue manager needs include the abilities to:

- Lead business revenue review meetings.
- Develop and deliver effective presentations.
- Establish credibility with the hotel's management team.
- Work closely with the director of sales and marketing on pricing (both short-term and long-term).
- Articulate complex strategies and other topics (both in oral and written format).

- Mentor and coach reservations and front desk personnel in revenue management strategies and tactics.
- Employ diplomatic skills to manage interpersonal conflicts.

Obviously, revenue managers need to be good with numbers, but, as you can see, their job entails a lot more than crunching numbers and producing reports. Revenue managers must be able communicators of the hotel's strategic and tactical revenue initiatives. They must be willing to take on a leadership role in helping build strong teams of co-workers committed to achieving revenue goals and business success.

The demands and expectations placed on revenue managers grow on a seemingly daily basis. However, in organizations that successfully embrace the challenges of sustainable growth, it is recognized that revenue management is not the job of a select few revenue management professionals. All of a hotel's revenue centers and support centers have to be on the same page in their understanding and support of common revenue goals. Revenue management is multifaceted, complex, and cross-disciplinary. Front-of-the house departments and back-of-the-house departments all have a part to play in helping a hotel maximize its revenue potential. It's the difficult job of the revenue manager to communicate the hotel's revenue management initiatives to, and coordinate them with, the rest of the hotel's staff.

References

AH&LA Educational Institute. 2005. *Certified Hospitality Revenue Manager Study Guide.*

The Basics of Revenue Management. 2005. Integrated Decisions and Systems, Inc. (IDeaS).

Burns, John, and Jon Inge. "Hold Your Horses! Getting a Grip on the Reins of Distribution Channel Management." *Hospitality Upgrade,* Summer 2004.

Gregory, Susan, and Jeffrey Beck. "The Activities, Training, and Reporting Relationships of Today's Revenue Managers." *HSMAI Marketing Review,* Fall 2006.

Appendix

Many of the items in this list of the top ten revenue management mistakes will be familiar to revenue management practitioners in the field who already bear some battle scars. However, some items may be new, so the list is offered in the hope that it might help revenue managers and others avoid some pitfalls. Smart people learn from their own mistakes; even smarter people learn from the mistakes of others.

The Top Ten Revenue Management Mistakes Hotels Make

10. Seeing revenue management as a job done only by the revenue manager.
9. Allowing Internet discounting agencies to sell guestrooms at prices of their choosing, then complaining about the erosion of rate integrity.
8. Claiming to differentiate the hotel based on service excellence, then promoting discounts, "value package" offerings, free frequent-guest points, and other freebies.
7. Thinking that the hotel's weekday strategy and weekend strategy can be the same.
6. Expecting that the "flag" (brand) will fill the hotel without the hotel's management team lifting a finger.
5. Counting revenue dollars as equal, regardless of the distribution channel they came through.
4. Thinking that short-term goals must always have priority over long-term goals.
3. Thinking that artificial intelligence—the revenue management software—is superior to human intelligence.
2. Believing that the right price to charge for a room night is established solely on the hotel's costs and ROI expectations.
1. Believing that discounting is an effective way to increase revenue.

What is actually meant by the above points? We will expand on these ideas in the following paragraphs, point by point.

Mistake 10: Seeing revenue management as a job done only by the revenue manager.

A husband helps his wife parallel park: "More to the right! Now backward! A lot more to the left! All the way! Forward! Now backward! A bit more!" Crunch! "Oh my! Now get out and see the damage *you've* done."

There are a number of hotel managers of different departments around the table at the revenue meetings when the topic of forecasts, inventory, and rate allocations are discussed. There is no shortage of opinions and advice.

Everybody has a point of view and feels compelled to contribute. Therefore, when all is said and done, it is not fair to single out the revenue manager if revenue goals are not met.

Revenue management success depends on the entire organization, and team efforts are required to achieve revenue objectives: "All for one and one for all" should be the watchword. The revenue manager can be the point person, but fingers should not be pointed and blame should not be assigned to a single individual or just one operational unit if revenue results are less than desired.

Mistake 9: Allowing Internet discounting agencies to sell guestrooms at prices of their choosing, then complaining about the erosion of rate integrity.

The industry's wakeup after 2003 on this issue was necessary and somewhat overdue. Until then, third-party Internet re-sellers used the merchant model to mark up room rates by 25–30 percent and were in control of sell rates. The hotel industry had nobody but itself to blame for this, and gradually the industry wrestled back control over room rates and distribution. The direct method of selling to guests using the hotel's own web portal may not be the highest revenue producer per reservation, but it is still the most cost efficient, most controllable, and yields the highest net room rate. The most important question at rate setting: Who is in charge?

Mistake 8: Claiming to differentiate the hotel based on service excellence, then promoting discounts, "value package" offerings, free frequent-guest points, and other freebies.

An incoming call to Excellent Service Hotel is put on hold and an automated voice system kicks in: "Your call is important to us. All of our agents are currently serving other callers. Please wait until the next available operator." And the message goes on for five more minutes in a loop. When the call is finally taken, a AAA discount of 10 percent is offered from the room rate without even verifying AAA membership. Go figure.

A hotel's strategic positioning should be the foundation of tactical rate management. Once a hotel decides to compete on service quality, location, unique selling points, or anything else but room rate, that positioning should be followed through with consistency. Competing on rates is a different game and it is not necessarily going to help a hotel's bottom line. A high-ranking executive of a global luxury chain known for its service excellence famously once said, "If we ever promote rate, we're dead." This blunt statement is a great example of consistency in brand message.

Discounts, freebies, and rate incentives may be quick fixes for disgruntled customers but they will not make up for lousy service or understaffed call centers. If service excellence is promised, that should be delivered, not discounts.

Mistake 7: Thinking that the hotel's weekday strategy and weekend strategy can be the same.

If the stay pattern, booking pattern, spending pattern, and market mix are different on weekdays than on weekends, at some point the hotel has to arrive at the logical conclusion that different strategies are needed on weekdays and weekends to maximize revenue. Hotel managers should base their decisions on solid data instead of wishful thinking. Different market dynamics warrant different strategic and tactical approaches for revenue maximization.

Mistake 6: Expecting that the "flag" (brand) will fill the hotel without the hotel's management team lifting a finger.

Hotel brands differ in terms of their marketing and other support. Some brands drive more revenue to their operators than others. Some brand marketing strategies, call centers, and web sites are better than others. However, even the best brand support cannot replace good operational care and close attention to guest service. Inattentive service staff, less-than-perfect cleanliness, and malfunctioning items (dead TV remote controls, broken hair driers, dripping faucets, thermostats that won't adjust room temperature, etc.) are not going to produce satisfied, loyal customers, no matter how well a brand promotes a destination. Hotel managers must own up to their responsibility regarding day-to-day operational issues, and they can't expect the brand to save a lousy product.

Mistake 5: Counting revenue dollars as equal, regardless of the distribution channel they came through.

Not all revenue dollars are created equal, because the costs associated with generating each revenue dollar can differ tremendously. Do the hotel's managers know what costs are associated with selling a room night through the hotel's corporate call center? The hotel's own website? A GDS channel? An e-merchant? A travel agent? A direct call from a return guest? An association?

There are various methods and channels a hotel can use to sell its products. Third parties are nice to have if they can fill rooms that the hotel cannot. Distribution channel management is now a core strategic competency. To play in the smartest way the hand a hotel is dealt requires an analysis of revenue production per distribution channel, plus an in-depth knowledge of the costs associated with each and every sales transaction. Commissions, switching-company costs, royalty fees, transaction charges, and other applicable costs need to be identified and compared.

Identical room rates paid by different guests may result in different net rates, based on a lot of cost variables that each hotel has to develop a solid understanding of. If more revenue comes through the least costly distribution channels, more profit is made without increasing occupancy.

Mistake 4: Thinking that short-term goals must always have priority over long-term goals.

Hotels are not for those who need to make a quick buck. Hotels are not built to last a few years. Hotels are built to last for decades, some for centuries. The hotel business is a marathon, not a sprint. There are high barriers to entry, it is a capital-intensive business, and its cost structure cannot be changed (most of a hotel's costs, being fixed, cannot be manipulated). Therefore, a long-term perspective is the only successful approach in the hotel business. It takes time to introduce a new property, build a clientele, and earn a solid reputation in the marketplace. Decision-makers should take all of this into consideration. Short-term thinking is not the way to long-term success, and the hotel industry shows no mercy to those who can't endure. When a short-term revenue objective conflicts with a hotel's long-term revenue and strategic goals, revenue managers must take a firm stand and never let short-term gains cause long-term pains.

Mistake 3: Thinking that artificial intelligence—the revenue management software—is superior to human intelligence.

By now we've all heard the modern-day adage, "To err is human—but to really foul things up, you need a computer." Computers are great tools in the decision-making process. They are fast and accurate, and by using extensive databases they can crunch a lot of variables in a short amount of time. However, sensible managers should always carefully check any results and not blindly follow the computers' lead. The system is not the solution and the media is not the message. Sometimes we mere humans do know better.

Sophisticated software products are of great help to managers, but they should not be asked to do what they were not designed to do. Binary logic works well but only up to a certain point. Humans have lateral-thinking capabilities, empathy, sensibility, and sensitivity, and can take the human element into consideration when making decisions. Managers know that guests are more than just room numbers, covers, or accounts. In short, decisions in a service-oriented business should be made by humans, not machines. Never let a computer run a hotel.

Mistake 2: Believing that the right price to charge for a room night is established solely on the hotel's costs and ROI expectations.

Good hotel managers know that the right price to charge for a guestroom is established by the market. Hotels should charge exactly what the market is able and willing to pay—not a dollar less, but not a dollar more. Today's savvy consumer will sniff out over-pricing in a heartbeat and will not hesitate to go after a better deal for a comparable product.

The twenty-first-century customer has comparison-shopping capability at his or her fingertips 24/7. Today's consumers have the ability to find the best value like never before, and nobody likes to overpay. Therefore, hotel managers must keep their fingers on the market's pulse, keep an ear close to the ground, and be on the ball at all times. Supply and demand dynamics can change quickly, and everybody wants to be the first to know. Does that mean hotel managers should constantly jerk room rates up and down in the name of dynamic pricing? Not at all. But it does mean they should always know what their product is worth. To help gauge that, managers should know what competitors are offering and what they are charging for it. Nothing can replace a thorough knowledge of the hotel's guests and how the hotel stacks up in a crowded market of comparable products. The danger of becoming a commodity is real, and inviting customers to choose only on price point reinforces their conviction that only the price really matters. If hotels have nothing else to offer, such customers will eventually be right.

Mistake 1: Believing that discounting is an effective way to increase revenue.

Smart hotel operators, who know they are selling an experience-based, intangible product—the hospitality experience at their properties—do not discount.

Several studies on hotel discounts concluded that discounts only generate partial results, and it is only the leisure segment which may react favorably. A fact: if downward pressures on room rates force hoteliers to discount heavily (examples: markets impacted by SARS, hurricanes, terrorist attacks, etc.), it takes several years to reach the same ADR than before the price decline started.

Discounts can only grab market share on a short-term basis. Customers who can be lured away from competitors as a result of lowering rates will generate cash flow but will not help profitability. Bargain-hunter customers who are willing to switch for a marginal price difference will always go where they can get a lower rate. This means that discounting in most cases will not improve RevPAR but will merely improve occupancy by getting the business of customers that nobody can retain, as they always will follow the cheapest deals available. Such customers are here today, gone tomorrow, based simply on which hotel has a special deal or which company is more desperate for cash.

Discounting can increase revenue and market share on a temporary basis, but it cannot increase hotel profits long-term. Most of the costs are fixed for a hotel. Lower room rates mean that a lot more units need to be sold, because the costs of capital, labor, utilities, and other items are not going to change. Lowering room rates may mean attracting a clientele that is not the one the hotel was built for, positioned to serve, or best equipped to satisfy. Those operators who meant to skim the cream at the top, only to one day find themselves scraping the bottom, know all too well the difference.

Discounting is not the only way to offer more value to customers. Before a rate decision is made in the face of softening demand, it is imperative to find out the reasons for the decline. Does it have anything to do with the product? With the competition? Are there economic, political, or health and safety issues behind it, independent from the hotel? Will a lower room rate help to ease those troubles? If there are other elements that can be bundled together with a room rate in order to create value for customers, can the rates be maintained?

It is not unusual to see a problem unrelated to room rates—for example, political uncertainty—cause a decrease in demand, and see hotels use lower room rates to solve it, as if a 50-percent discount could suddenly provide the illusion of safety and security (to continue with our political uncertainty example) at a destination hit by political instability and turmoil or the danger of terrorist attacks. There are no easy answers and quick fixes for such problems.

Hotels have to have realistic expectations about prices and know which issues are price-related and which are not. There are a lot of trigger-happy revenue managers eager to pull the rate trigger and unleash a variety of discounts instead of adjusting the hotel's products and working harder to get the business a hotel needs to meet its revenue targets.

Rates are too important to be used as the first line of defense. Instead, rates should be the last line of defense, turned to only after every other avenue has been exhausted. Even then, rates should be adjusted with a great deal of care.

Index